DON'T WORRY, IT GETS WORSE

Lily Cummings

ALIDA NUGENT is the creator of *The Frenemy*, a female-centric comedy blog that is devoted to making weird girls feel good about themselves. Since its creation over three years ago, it has appeared on *The Huffington Post*, *Thought Catalog*, *Gothamist*, *HelloGiggles*, *Refinery 29*, and crumb-filled laptops everywhere. A graduate of Emerson College, Nugent majored in writing and is as shocked as you are that, in this economy, she is able to find a living doing that. She currently resides in Brooklyn, where she stares at dogs and eats sandwiches on stoops and isn't in a band. This is her first book.

don't worry, it gets worse

One Twentysomething's (Mostly Failed) Attempts at Adulthood

Alida Nugent

A PLUME BOOK

PLUME
Published by the Penguin Group
Penguin Group (USA) Inc., 375 Hudson Street,
New York, New York 10014, USA

USA | Canada | UK | Ireland | Australia | New Zealand | India | South Africa | China
Penguin Books Ltd, Registered Offices: 80 Strand, London WC2R 0RL, England
For more information about the Penguin Group visit penguin.com

First published by Plume, a member of Penguin Group (USA) Inc., 2013

P REGISTERED TRADEMARK—MARCA REGISTRADA

LIBRARY OF CONGRESS CATALOGING-IN-PUBLICATION DATA
Nugent, Alida.
Don't worry, it gets worse : one twentysomething's (mostly failed) attempts at
adulthood / Alida Nugent.
pages cm
ISBN 978-0-452-29818-7 (pbk.)
1. Young adults—Humor. 2. Adulthood—Humor. I. Title
PN6231.A26N84 2013
818'.602—dc23   2012049144

Printed in the United States of America
10 9 8 7 6 5 4 3 2

Set in Bembo Std.
Designed by Leonard Telesca

Penguin is committed to publishing works of quality and integrity. In that spirit, we are proud to offer
this book to our readers; however, the story, the experiences, and the words are the author's alone.

To my mother, my mamita, my maaa,
the woman who showed me how strong and tough and kind
a female could be. Thanks for believing in me above all else—
this book is proudly for you. I love you more than a
grinch like me can express.

Contents

contents

Introduction

A Survey: Is This Book for You?

Here's how it works: If you answer yes to ten or more questions, then you should read this book. If you don't, then buy it anyway and give it to the coolest person you know. This author needs money to eat her feelings.

1. Does your college degree hang over your head like a rain cloud made of student loans, false hopes, and rapidly fading dreams?
2. Is feeling enormous panic when you think about your life a normal, everyday occurrence? Is this panic heightened by the smell of Axe body spray when you enter a bar? The thought of people asking about your future? The fear of missing your favorite television show?
3. Do you handle this panic by drinking?
4. Not heavily, just a bottle of wine on Wednesday? You

might as well finish the whole bottle because you opened it with your teeth?

5. Would you rather feast on hummus or cheese than have sex with somebody who doesn't read books, drinks protein shakes, or has a goatee?

6. Can you name at least twelve to fifteen of the Real Housewives with great pride and organized by the kind of medication they take?

7. But can you still remain up-to-date on the news and current events?

8. Have you had more imaginary relationships with celebrities, text relationships, or relationships with common house cats than relationships with real people?

9. If I were to sing "Everybody (yeah)," would you automatically respond with "Rock your body?"

10. Do late-night Food Network television shows put you in a lifeless trance?

11. Have you thought about the Internet longingly when you were not near it today?

12. Jon Hamm?

13. Are you very, very afraid to walk in heels?

14. Have you been wearing dirty sweatpants this whole time?

15. Would you like to burn all the magazines that use the word *member* or *johnson* as synonyms for *penis*?

16. Have you sorted yourself into a Hogwarts house yet?

17. Liz Lemon?

18. Is your greatest battle with your hair?
19. If you're single, is that okay?
20. Do you ever feel like you're the last girl in the world who is the way she is?

Thank you! If you haven't closed this book yet, I'm assuming you have passed this test and are worthy of reading it. Good! *It's the last test you'll ever take.*

Because I am being forced to talk about myself throughout this whole book, you might as well get to know the basics about me. My name is Alida, which I hope you have discerned by now. I am not famous, I am not photogenic, I am not dating a celebrity, I am not the child of a celebrity, and I am not on television. I'm also not very good at closing blinds or opening jars without assistance. I am a human being who likes writing and puppies and sandwiches. In fact, I'm also a twentysomething who finds some Justin Bieber songs rather catchy. So how did I get here, writing a book on real paper and not just in my head full of pipe dreams? Short answer: dumb luck. Another short answer: My feverish love for the World Wide Web and writing and my postcollege joblessness compelled me to start a blog called *The Frenemy*. That blog became popular on *Tumblr*, just enough for me to write this book, where I talk about a lot of the things I love, a lot of the things I hate, and all of the things I want. I like to make fun of myself in this book. You'll see why. I'm a big ole weirdo who enjoys the finer things in life: staying home on Saturday nights watching basic cable, molding boyfriends out of ice cream, and painting my nails and smearing them within minutes. I assume you understand.

A few years ago, I graduated college, diploma in one hand, margarita in the other, completely oblivious to the shit storm that was coming my way. Here's a preview: becoming a living, breathing, job-having, bill-paying, responsible adult? Really fucking difficult. I know every old person you ever meet says it's so easy to be in your twenties now, what with our lack of world wars and easy access to Jamba Juice and our constant stream of devilish rock music. But I beg to differ. For some people, being in your twenties is a time of exploration and sex and going on millions of dates and having your parents pay for shit. I don't see it that way. For me, it's a time of rolling around and watching my life moments get devoured whole by the Internet, all while hoping I eventually figure out both my future and how to make my hair look nice. It's hard, but not in a way that you feel like you have any right to complain about it, which makes it even harder.

I'm going to level with you here. I am not going to give you one of those speeches where I say "I *am* you" because that always has a creepy "the call is coming from the *house*" horror movie vibe and I don't like that. I am not you. Sure, we all put on our pajamas the same way—one leg at a time and in front of our televisions with chips pouring out of our mouth—but that doesn't mean we are all similar organisms. However, I know that I can't be the only one out there trying to figure out how to navigate the choppy waters of adulthood. In fact, to give you another nautical analogy . . . being in your twenties is like being on a nice boat, but instead of drinking champagne and hanging out with cast members of the *Real World*, you're on the deck underneath a tarp, rocking back and forth and drooling. I want to lift that tarp for myself, and for you, too. All I can do is share some of my experiences with you and hope you relate to them, laugh at them, feel pity for them, whatever. Really, I want you to finish this book feeling like we could become friends, if the timing was right. That's it.

Oh, and by the way, you should drink while you're reading this book. If you want to play a drinking game, I suggest you take a shot when you feel like I am abusing commas. Or when I reference a reality show you like to watch. Or when I make a joke you particularly like. Or whenever you want to take a shot, really. No judgment.

So that's me. Keep on readin' if you want to hear about stuff you might already be experiencing. Is that cool? Are you busy? You wanna hang out for a bit?

ALIDA

don't worry, it gets
worse

Once I Was a Baby

If you ever find yourself in possession of a time machine, do yourself a favor and go back in time and punch your childhood self between one and thirty times in the face. All right, I actually hate it when people say, "If you had a time machine," because, like, *what, where, how?* Do you realize what a serious responsibility that would be? You'd have to weigh all of the options of how you could alter the fabric of history and time. It's great power *and* great responsibility, a burden only previously given to Tobey Maguire and Andrew Garfield as Spider-Mans. You'd also *have* to say that you would go back and kill Hitler. Fine. Go ahead and shoot that asshole in the neck, and then fulfill your other mission: punching your childhood self in the face.

All right, I know it sounds cruel that I'm advocating violence and also maybe violence to kids, but hear me out. This is a *self-preservation* tactic. You're gonna punch your kid-self in the face to straighten 'em out, so that he or she doesn't grow up to be a person with insane ambitions, which, if you're like me, you definitely had as a child. *Nothing* good can come from having lofty dreams as a kid. It's the first step to becoming something truly awful, like a person who thinks everybody cares about your vacation photographs or the type who wants to be a motivational speaker. You gotta nip this in the bud. You gotta hit yourself and say, "Kid-self, I demand you to decrease the size of your dreams, and I demand you to take note that your shit stinks, and I demand you to say no when Benjamin Carpenter asks you out in high school." Punch the kid again, then give 'em a stern finger point. "CONTROL YOUR DREAMS." Poof. You're gone. Back in time to go fuck up some slave owners.

In this day and age, big dreams are the first step down a long, lonely path to disappointment and everybody hating you. Medium-size dreams are okay. Small dreams are fine. Big dreams? Big dreams are for people who eventually wear Sperry Top-siders and refer to themselves as "the Future Spielberg." If my lame little cereal-eating monster-self didn't grow up thinking life was all Cheerios and cuddles, I might have done something sensible, like become a stockbroker or an economist or, at the very least, a person who reads the newspaper or works out in the morning. Instead, I grew up thinking I could make money by telling jokes and writing them down. If that isn't a straight shot to poverty, I don't know what it is. Big dreams for Alida "the Dumbass" Baby.

Whenever someone brings up the traits associated with being a functional human otherwise known as an "adult," I think, is this even possible for me? Probably not, is what I conclude. I mean, I'll eventually pay off my college loans at the age of forty-five by selling what's left of my liver, and I'll probably manage to find sustenance and remember to breathe oxygen constantly. I'll *survive*. However, for people like me, it's going to be a long, hard road of playing "How much dip can go on this chip," "How many minutes have gone listlessly by," "HOW SAD IS TOO SAD?!" There will be years of struggling to keep myself afloat. I'm sure I will have to murder between one and fifty bill collectors. I'm certain I'll have to go to Vegas to turn tricks. (I'm sorry, *illusions*, *Gob*!) All for what? Stupid jokes? A burning desire to be a writer? Congratulations on your feelings, delicate little Emily Dickinson Jr. You know, she was a recluse because she smelled bad and couldn't afford to be anything else. Great role model.

My lofty ambitions are partially due to the fact that I'm a member of Generation "Yes You Can, I Guess: How about I throw a combination of money, attention, and prescription medication at the problem?" Anyone born during the years 1983–1990 is screwed right along with me. Our generation didn't get to experience all the fun and joy of the 1980s. We didn't get the huge cell phones, the suspender-wearing yuppie greediness, or the mixed tapes. We got the aftermath of people being so exhausted by a decade filled with cocaine and assassinations and Ronald Reagan that they forgot to say, "Oh yeah, we should keep our children in line and guide them to have realistic expectations of life." The pop culture of the time even proves it:

How the 1980s
Screwed Over This Generation

1. *The Cosby Show*: *The Cosby Show* showed parents that they should start paying attention to their kids and be really, really supportive of them all of the time. If we were born in the '60s or '70s, our parents would be too busy smoking weed or discoing to even notice whether we were still alive. But the Cosbys put on some comfy fucking sweaters and lovingly parented the shit out of their brood, and so your parents did, too. They also taught parents that their kids could be really alternative and against the grain and feminist like Lisa Bonet's character, and they would still find a way to love them anyway.

2. *Pretty in Pink*: This movie showed parents that it was totally cool for their girls to be socially maladjusted weirdos. Molly Ringwald made dresses out of *curtains*, for Christ's sake, and she still ended up with what looked like the most stable, rich seventeen-year-old in America. Apparently, all parents had to do was allow their kids to do what they were passionate about, and, in turn, they could be drunk and unemployed like the father in that movie. It would all work out!

3. Madonna: Hey, it's totally okay with your daughter being sort of skanky because it will make her millions of dollars!

4. MTV: Just another ideal for your kids to aspire to, parents! Now that they have constant access to rock stars and their

glamorous, drugged-out sex lives, your children will want to become one more than ever! All this constant exposure will lead them to become part of a band that will never make it, or to have sex with someone in a band that will never make it. Doesn't that make you feel good for exposing your kids to Music Television at an early age?

5. *Dallas*: The show that your parents watched instead of watching you—meanwhile, we were learning air guitar and fashioning cone breasts out of paper plates and smoking pretzel sticks like cigarettes.

SUMMARY: Parents should be supportive of their weird, slutty kids, because even if they don't end up okay, they'll probably get their own television shows.

Let's face it: Parents have gotten too soft, too sensitive, too unwilling to let their kid know they just might fail. Every parent these days cheers their offspring on like they're the only kid on the middle school honor roll. Gone are the days of adolescents being pressured by their parents to take over the family business. ("But, *Dad*, I don't want to be like you!") Gone are the days of girls dressing conservatively and choosing to become secretaries or typists. Gone are the good ole days of promised, unsatisfactory employment! (Well, not the good ole days in terms of the overt racism and the poodle skirts and the shock therapy, but you know what I'm sayin'.)

Now the prevailing parenting philosophy is that you should let your kids do what makes them happy. Guess what, parents? Happiness doesn't buy shit, and, one day, your kids are gonna want some shit. What you need to do is say, "Hey, offspring, you might not be able to fly, but you're going to make excellent middle management someday." That's better encouragement!

How in the world did *I* ever get the idea that I should *follow my dreams* in the first place? Sorry to say, but you gotta point your finger at my parents. I love my parents, I really do, but sometimes I have to question why they raised me to believe in myself. Simply put, they gave me too much self-esteem. I was a *dumb* kid, but a grand old cheer erupted whenever I managed to grasp a simple concept without fucking up the whole thing. I gave all the ladies in my coloring books purple skin, and my parents were ecstatic when I didn't shit out a crayon at the end of the day. I thought that I would have absolutely no problem conquering the world on a dinosaur as the first firefighting ballerina; I watched Lamb Chop and thought it was perfectly reasonable that a crazy ginger lived in the forest with a bunch of socks that she put false eyelashes on; I'd run around finger painting and watching princess movies and was told all the time, "You can, you can!" Not once did anybody say that I was out of my tiny fucking mind. My parents thought it was adorable that I ran around screaming, which is pretty much the only reason why performance art exists in the first place.

I mean, really. Look at some of my childhood dreams, and

see whether you can spot "a lifetime of stability and happiness." (Spoiler alert: you won't.)

A Comprehensive List of My Childhood Dreams

Comedian: The other day, I found a joke book I wrote in when I was six and in it, it said, "JOKES: How did the elephant climb the ladder? With great difficulty." That's. Not. Funny. Yet my parents laughed their checkbooks away.

Writer: In fourth grade, we had to write fables for our final projects. I wrote one entitled "How the Chow Chow Got Its Blue Tongue." Chow chows are fat dogs that have blue tongues, in case you didn't know. I knew, as a kid, because I had a magazine subscription to *Dog Fancy*. The story I so carefully crafted was a tale of terrible child abuse—a cruel dog-father who, when his son "acted out," would shove him in a freezer. One day, when the dog-child did something that I don't remember but probably was something like "protecting his mother," the dad left him there to freeze. The dog emerged with a blue tongue and became an expensive toy for very rich people.

That story is pretty fucked up. What is more fucked up is that I named the puppy's father after *my* dad, because I couldn't think of another name. My dad has never laid a hand on me, which is something that my fourth-grade teacher could never quite believe.

Hallmark card girl: You know those jokey birthday cards that wives give their husbands when they secretly hate them? The ones with the picture of a "hot" girl on the front that says something like, "This girl wants a BIG part of you on your birthday," or whatever else insinuates that this lady wants a penis, and then when you open the card it says, "Kidding, you're a fat, disgusting slob," or whatever else insinuates that the lady who gave you the card wants a divorce? I remember being a kid and looking at one with my mother while she was looking for a card for hopefully not my father. On it was a girl who had a white one-piece bathing suit, Tiffani-Amber Thiessen hair, and harlotlike makeup. I wanted to be her so badly, because she looked very worldly and special to me. I thought I would look good on those kinds of cards, helping a husband and wife continue down their dark road of marital hell. I went home and smeared makeup on my face like Buffalo Bill.

Witch: This is pretty self-explanatory, but I wanted to be a witch when I was younger. I was never sure which side I was on. Good-witch-wise, I wanted to be Sabrina and travel through linen closets and date a guy with one earring and talk to a cat all day. Bad-witch-wise, I would have enjoyed being Sarah Jessica Parker in *Hocus Pocus* and killing children all day.

Can we say, "Headed toward a liberal arts degree and also writing a sign about how I have a degree as I beg for change on the subway"? Yet, throughout the years of these absurd dreams, my parents were incredibly supportive. They liked my "little stories." They liked them so much they gave me the chutzpah to like those stories, too, and to chase that dream of becoming a writer. Screw you, Mom and Dad! (I love you, Mom and Dad.)

When I got older and realized that my life was built around the idea that my career would be something I wanted to love, to strive for, to be proud of, I was scared. I know I'm not the only one. A lot of my friends had passions, too—they wanted to be filmmakers or brain surgeons or fashion designers, and all because nobody told them no. Well, friends, here goes a whole lot of years of trouble. There's no time machine to go back and make us into reasonable creatures. We're romantic. We're hopeful. We're done for. The worst part of this all? The idea of struggle and compromise seems *exciting* to us—that's how stupid we are. There's no stopping fools, I say. We're still kids at heart. Those dreams are still there. Now we just have to go chase them.

And now, we've started running.

If You Want to Keep Your Dignity Intact, Stay Away from Tequila

One day, I will become the kind of adult who can throw a *real* party, I think as I take my top off in front of a small group of friends and acquaintances. *One day.*

How did I get to that moment? No, I was not trying out as an extra for *Showgirls 2: Also Not Sexy Boogaloo*. Nor was I so angry at my dad I used his credit card to go to Cancun for spring break.

This is a story of girl meets tequila.

Let's rewind. A week before this sad striptease, I had marched into the kitchen with the kind of idea that stemmed from summer boredom and reading *Good Housekeeping* at the doctor's office. My roommate Brittanie sat eating her signature salad of June 2010: this slop *thing* of tuna, black beans, raw onions, and shredded cheese. To me, it posed the question, Is a salad simply a salad because it is cold, healthy, and disgusting, or does it also need to have lettuce and be disgusting? Brittanie looked at me expectantly, her adorable cheeks marred by the demon's lunch food.

I stood in front of her, eyes blazing defiantly, stubby little legs doing a weird jig that only comes out whenever I have true moments of genius.

"BRITTANIE. Let's have a *party*. A really CLASSY, ADULT party."

I waved my arms wildly, words racing a mile a minute, saying things like, "We're gonna go all out" and "Let's see what Martha Stewart has to say on the subject of decorative napkins." I explained my plan with a level of enthusiasm that would make you think *nobody had ever hosted a party before*. I was a genius, a revolutionary on par with whoever invented those low-calorie wedges of cheese.

I had hosted many a shindig before, but those seemed to serve only as warnings to insubordinate youth, with me as the ball-and-chained apparition: the Ghost of College Parties Past. Imagine me, wearing the standard college uniform of UGG boots and a North Face jacket, haunting your local bar that doesn't ID—"Hey, kid, you think college is all fun and games? I'll tell you what, it kind of is. But watch what happens when you host a party in your decrepit, mouse-ridden apartment, the one that houses eight people and constantly smells like your roommate's cooking mistakes. Yeah, and because you're so smart, have everyone guzzle down Four Loko, the type that has both caffeine *and* alcohol. You wanna hear what happens? You gotta clean twice. Once before the party, and once for the vomit afterward. Good times, though."

The last fete I had hosted descended into the type of debauchery that even a "cool mom" who lets you have wine coolers at barbecues would warn her kids against. By the night's end, the following things may or may not have happened:

1. A bunch of guys who were really into metal music showed up uninvited and drank inhuman amounts of beer, leading one to piss in the corner of the living room.
2. One of my usually very responsible roommates tried coke (drug, not soda) and ran around the house until I had to chase her with a broom. (KIDS: DON'T DO DRUGS.)
3. More than one couple ended up having sex in the bathtub; no fewer than three people were found crying in closets.
4. The birthday girl's iPod got stolen and my roommate had his hookah smashed to pieces. Who would smoke there now?
5. I drank so much caffeinated alcohol that I began to collect and count all of the beer bottles, until finally I had had enough and pretended that the cops were coming. (Note: Do this at a party where everyone is heavily intoxicated and watch the chaos that ensues.)

Needless to say, much like my collection of various bodysuits I own and never wear, I had no idea how to pull off a party. However, as a newly minted college grad, I was feeling the pressure to enter Adult World and envisioned this party to be a "coming-out ball" for my latent maturity. Frankly, living alone without electrocuting myself sounded daunting enough. (I mean, really, you're looking at someone who barely passed Latin American Culture Through Film aka movie watching 101.) But I reasoned that I could tackle hosting a mature party more easily than, say, trying to make conversation with a guy who had a job in finance over small plates of garlic shrimp (the most mature thing I can think of). So a party it was. That's what I would do in my slow climb to owning pairs of smart heels.

After hearing my passionate defense of how we had to grow up and live life without doing keg stands, Brittanie agreed to be my cohost for this elegant affair. We carefully selected the friends who we deemed most deserving of this shindig that was meant to be remembered "fondly but not epically." This was not a *woooo*, what-a-crazy-night kind of party; this was meant to be a wasn't-that-a-nice kind of evening. Yeah, I said evening. We settled on men who were fashionably gay or considered gay by society because of their sharp sweater collection, and ladies who had never thrown up rum in front of us.

In light of the whole "making this an evening and not a frat party," gone were those days of inviting people to parties via Facebook invitations with a picture of a girl flat down on her panties. No, instead, I made the bold choice to call our esteemed guests, with a Madonna-British accent, and cordially invited them to our place on Saturday at 8 P.M. sharp. It was clear to everyone that this was going to be "cat eating out of glass goblet in those cat food commercials" fancy. To really push the point home, I made it clear that the requested attire was "Look good enough to get laid, but really, this isn't that type of party. Come on, can't you have fun without having to have sex with somebody? Jesus."

After getting several enthusiastic yeses from our gals and gays and not-quite gays, it was time to dream up how our fancy-ass party would look. This was my time to shine, to put Martha Stewart to shame. I imagined immaculate canapés, the kinds that were featured on the Triscuit box. I would walk well in said smart heels, serving said canapés on a silver platter. My cohost, thankfully, had more realistic expectations. After living together for three years, Brittanie was both my partner in crime and the one bringing me back down to reality when I needed it. And she did not hold back when it came to stomping on my party-planning dreams, as evidenced by a snippet of our pre-party debates:

Me: "How about we try to make ice sculptures? Like, if we bought a block of ice and got a hammer, we could hack at it until it resembled the Empire State Building. Maybe ice sculptures of each of our guests in various patriotic poses?"

Brittanie: "Do you even own a hammer?"

Me: "All right, all right, all right. How do you feel about real silverware?"

Brittanie: "I feel fine about it. Do you have any?"

Me: "What about having a fondue fountain?"

Brittanie: "You know we're going to use that once and then it'll sit under the sink with hardened cheese on it. You know we're not going to clean that thing."

Oh yeah, speaking of cleaning. This was a step I was trying to avoid. Having a neat house to reside in should have probably been a logical part of getting my shit together, but just thinking about the act of cleaning makes me want to take a nap with a Brillo pad as a pillow. There wasn't anything in the rule books that said mature people were supposed to have clean houses, anyway. I'd seen *Hoarders* enough to know that lots of adults didn't clean. But on the other hand, I'd also seen *Hoarders* enough to know I didn't want to be the kind of adult who had only cat skeletons for friends. We would have to spruce up the place up before we had everyone over. So two days before the party, I put on my best impression of the action hero rallying the group of criminal misfits to save the day and said, "Hey, let's do this!"

Do you want to know the easiest way to tell if somebody is a human being who can function well in society or is an idiot baby who lives in a state of filth? Open up their fridge. Specifically, look at their vegetable drawers. Go on, do it, but put on a hazmat suit first if you suspect it of being less than sparkling. I know this because I made the unfortunate decision to examine mine and was surprised to find *gunk* at the bottom of it. It looked like soy sauce, but given its location, it was more likely from the red peppers that were bought approximately one month ago. I had planned on making a hearty stir fry, but all things must pass. Now, the peppers were fermenting into some sort of noxious mold that was probably attacking and eating my brain for days on end.

And it wasn't just the vegetable drawers. This is something that I probably should have learned at an early age, but apparently condiments have expiration dates? I'm just as surprised as you are to know that something as delicious as ranch dressing could expire. Maybe it's because I usually just put a straw in my ranch dressing and slurp it down in one gulp before the light of the next day can hit it. Regardless, kids, do yourself a favor and check those salad dressings.

After hours of using all of the Swiffers and scrubby things we had available, the kitchen actually looked kind of decent. Brittanie and I threw up our arms in victory, until we realized that we couldn't make our lunch in there or else it would *destroy everything*. We marched to our bedrooms to ride the cleaning high, which is, I assume, like a meth high, if doing meth makes you feel like a housewife who has inhaled all of the fumes of her cleaning products.

Slowly but surely, our shit was coming together. The afternoon of the party, Brittanie went over all of the details. Semiclean house? Check. Decorations? One lone candle and a throw pillow for the win! Food that wasn't just chips poured into a bowl five minutes before guest arrivals? Check, but only because Brittanie made stuffed mushrooms, which I wouldn't touch because, let's be real, mushrooms taste like dirt. Now, for the drink making. We were going to be providing guests with libations because I wanted to be the kind of person who doesn't squawk BYOB into the eardrums of everybody for at least one night. I wanted to seem generous, kind of like the bird lady from *Home Alone 2*, but instead of dumping birdseed in front of pigeons, I would be providing alcohol to pour down the mouths of my friends. So in the spirit of that, I bought cheap-ass tequila and steeped jalapeño peppers in sugar syrup for hours, trying to make true to my promise that we would have jalapeño-infused margaritas. Looking back, I guess we technically did. But I didn't own a blender or buy any ice, so we had a lukewarm something or other that I put too much Triple Sec in because I was proud that I had bought Triple Sec. That shit is expensive and you can't even drink it in shot form, but "SO IT GOES."

Right before everyone arrived, we added some final touches to make this get to Giada De Laurentiis-elegant-but-still-a-mini-meatball-platter level. We sprayed Febreze almost everywhere. We had a record player that didn't work, so instead we put some Billie Holiday on the computer and put that *behind* the record player. It was all ambience-and-fancy-Christmas-lights awesome, and I was pretty sure I deserved a Nobel Peace Prize or *Time's* Lady of the Year for it. And because a hostess has to look sexy, I had put peacock feathers in my hair, for "Westchester Technical High School Presents *A*

Midsummer Night's Dream" chic. I looked like the fanciest of idiots—an idiot who was growing up!

Ten people showed up, which is the perfect "not a rager, just a nice get-together, with you know, the group" size. Everything was going so well. Witness a conversation that just screams "mature partygoers."

Me, standing in the corner in heels, because I continued to wear heels in the house for the sound they made on the tiles: "Brad, as a vegetarian, do you know that you almost certainly have a B12 deficiency? I hope you're taking supplements." I push a plate of mushrooms toward him.

"Not as often as I should. . . ." Brad munches on one of the provided mushroom caps, hoping that these three bites will make up for his dearth of nutrients.

"Yes, you're probably dying at this very moment because you don't have enough B12. Or it might just make you lose your hair. I'm too short to tell if that's starting to happen already, even with these heels on. Here, come to my cabinet. I keep vitamins in the same cabinet I keep my spices, but don't worry, I've almost never gotten them confused." We walk across the kitchen, and I put vitamins in a small Ziploc bag.

"Why thank you, Alida. Would you like to talk about global politics? Or some literature, perhaps?" He adjusts his smart cashmere sweater as the music changes to Ella Fitzgerald. I take another small sip of tequila.

"Brad, that would be lovely!"

End scene.

Setting aside the fact that my mature conversational attempts made me sound like I was the kind of pretentious ass who says she watches *films* and not movies, there was one glaring problem with that scenario: tequila, and my sipping on it. Tequila is God of Throwing Up Everything Ever Stored in Your Intestines Ever and Also Making You an Insane Person. It knows no age, race, gender, religion. It is an equal-opportunity, ruin-your-night alcohol. And we were all drinking it.

Let's face the facts: Nobody right out of college is used to handling their liquor. Up until then, we were accustomed to the evolution of college drinking—going from very obviously sneaking sips of vodka out of water bottles to drinking two-dollar beers at whatever bar wouldn't card to actually being legal age but still stupid enough to make a fool out of yourself no less than 50 percent of the time when out drinking. We were not yet at the point to be responsible enough to bring a bottle of wine to somebody's apartment to be consumed by at least three people. We were still amateurs. This became abundantly clear when we went from casually sipping on my margarita inventions to doing rounds of shots. I'm sure they were dignified shots. I'm sure we did them in real-glass shot glasses, and I'm sure we toasted to economic upturn. But once you start doing shots of tequila, you're entering a vortex from which you will never return.

After the third shot, Brad dropped a mushroom cap. I swear this happened in slow motion—the mushroom spinning slowly on the floor like a top or dreidel, depending on your faith. From that point on, the mood of the room started to change. The adults were gone, replaced with the childish monsters we really were. Somebody changed the old-timey music to something more hip. The Christmas lights started flickering ominously. It's eleven o'clock, do you know where your children are? They were right here, ready to have the kind of Saturday night where twentysomethings would act like their natural selves: animals.

The lot of us reconvened to the living room, where somebody pulled out a deck of cards. Who pulls out a deck of cards at a party? Answer: either very old people or very young people. This thing was taking a Slip'N Slide right into the Dane Cook depths of a college party, and I could do nothing to stop it.

The cards were drawing us to their collegiate siren song, and people started throwing out suggestions left and right, the beats of Ke$ha blaring in the background.

"Let's play beer pong with GLASSES!"

"No, no, let's play flip cup!"

"We should play kings!"

You know kings, right? The game where you sit in a circle and every card picked out of the deck meant somebody drinks and everybody loses all sense of dignity? Brittanie and I shared a look of panic. Kings was *not* the direction we wanted this party to take. I was not going to spend thirty minutes arguing whether or not pulling a queen card meant we had to ask each other questions or take a shot. I had PTSD flashbacks of a rowdy game of "Never have I ever . . ." where everybody found out I had shaved my face because I heard that's what exfoliated it just as well as expensive scrubs. However, kings was child's play compared to the next suggestion:

"How about strip poker?"

... Because, clearly, that was the most mature thing we could surmise to do with the cards. Definitely worked with my party theme of "Ann Taylor Gets Her Groove Back."

Much to my chagrin, the crowd responded to this with a resounding chorus of "Yeaaahhhhhhhhhhhh, okay!" Enthusiasm! It shall be done!

You know how everyone has one of those friends who has no problem walking around naked around the locker room? Yeah, that's not me. I've never skinny-dipped, I don't flash people for fun, and the only time I don't wear a bra is when I'm wearing an incredibly sexy giant T-shirt with a dog on it. I am not uncomfortable with my body, but I've never reveled in it like a woman in a bodywash advertisement. However, on this night, with my stupid feather in my hair and my tequila drink in hand, I agreed to strip poker. Potential reasons why I agreed to abandon my strict antinakedness policies are as follows:

1. I'm a complete egomaniac who thinks she can win every game she ever plays.
2. If I was going to keep the last vestiges of hope that this was an adult party, strip poker seemed like the kind of thing that forty-year-old couples do on their trip to Bermuda when they are too scared to become swingers.

I should also mention that I (of course) have absolutely *no idea how to play poker.* I think the only time I've ever been exposed to poker is that painting of those anthropomorphic, card-slinging dogs. Ironically, I had a strategy without even knowing it: I wear about thirty-five layers at all times, regardless of season, and on this particular night, it included tights, a vest, a tank top, and a high-waisted skirt. But layers work only so well if you know how to play the game, and I started to lose almost immediately. And as the following conversation illustrates, I am not very good at losing:

> Friend 1: "Alida, you lost. Take your top off."
> Me: "I'd rather not. Let me go to my bedroom for a sec, I forgot to feed my bird."
> Friend 2: "You don't have a bird."
> Me: "What? You know *nothing* about me."
> (Goes to room, stands there a second, leaves room.)
> Friend 2 (eyes rolling): "You are now wearing socks over your stockings."
> Me: "No, I always do this. This house is unseasonably cold for June."
> Friends 1–10: "Come on! Take something off!"
> Me: "I will take off my stockings and leave the socks or my one of two hats. Your choice."

But it wasn't just me. This particular game of strip poker was the most morose game of cards I ever played. Every card pulled was met with dead eyes. Shirts were taken off with a lack of enthusiasm seen only with golf audiences. Brittanie's dress came off with the kind of "Fuck it, I knew this would happen anyway" attitude of a cynical divorcée after her first failed relationship. Why were we intent on playing? I'm not sure. But nobody wanted to be the nerd who ended the enlightened gathering of "adults."

As cards were thrown down and clothes were becoming scarcer and scarcer, people started to realize: Need. More. Booze. But because we had started the night off by drinking like wild animals, the supply was dwindling. My friend Ian began to swig Triple Sec from the bottle, frantically trying to get drunk on the sugar and minimal alcohol content. We all began pouring whatever liquor was left from the bottles straight into our mouths, perhaps contemplating if we should just smash them and lick the glass shards. The greatest fear among us was not being naked—it was the idea that we could become sober and clearly remember each other's body parts.

Do you know how weird it is to sit next to the guy who you really like as a friend, but who used to sleep with your best friend, so you kind of already know what he looks like naked, when he's almost completely naked? Well, I kept side-eyeing him for one thing, because it's not like my friend hadn't described what he *looked like*. AWKWARD.

There was a lot of silence in that room. Everybody was shrugging or frowning and desperately trying to avoid making accidental eye contact with any flaccid penises. This wasn't fun, this was *painful*.

Finally, I cleared my throat.

"So . . . I'm not wearing any clothes, really. Does anybody even know how to fucking play poker? At all???" I was being honest.

Brittanie started to laugh. Next, I started to laugh, mostly because I was still wearing a skirt and a bra, so there was victory on my end. Soon, everybody was laughing, their naked parts flapping around. This was when I decided to take off my bra.

"You know," I said, "just because we're not in college anymore doesn't mean we can't get a little *crazy*!"

Brittanie chimed in, "Yeah, I mean, I *know* we live in this fantastically clean apartment with all these Christmas lights . . . but your hosts know how to let loose!"

I flung my sensible bra at her sensible head as we all sat around nodding about how we were so obviously adults now, but cool adults who could do wild things like take off their clothes at parties. We were cultured and smart, we agreed, but we knew how to keep our youth alive and our bodies visible while we still had them. Were we *not* just talking about health, vitality, and philosophy? Were we *not* just eating crudités and discussing various intelligent books? Of course we were! However, by no means were we straitlaced. We could really unstring the corsets, lest you forget it! Discussing this felt better for all of us, really, and our guests gathered their boxers and shirts and skirts and left me by my clean kitchen sink, the last gulps of Triple Sec dribbling from my chin onto the floor.

"We promise never to talk about this again," we all agreed as everyone left. Adults, after all, are the kind of people who keep quiet. Adults are the kind of people who have parties and never tell anybody of the slipups they made at them. We would only allude to this one night at future bar outings with tiny nods of acknowledgment. It was an unmarked day in history: the time we all grew up and became comfortable with our youthful nakedness. We would always remain silent.

Until now. Sorry, guys.

The Apple Doesn't Fall Far from the Tree

When I called my mother to tell her I was moving home, it had been a long time coming. She knew it was going to happen. I knew it was going to happen. It was just a matter of me coming to terms with the inevitable, like someone receiving a prison sentence.

"It will only be for a little while," I told her. "Just until I get a job." Everybody nodded and tried to cover up their hysterical laughter at the lie we all knew I was telling.

I had been avoiding the inevitable by crafting the typical postcollege vision board, complete with a rapid timeline to success and the kind of delirious insanity that would have me owning a "starter home" with my "starter dog" by age twenty-eight. I kept telling everybody I was going to move to Austin, Texas, after graduation because of its cheap living, delicious Mexican food, and because I could wear sundresses all year-round. Never mind the fact that I had no money and no job there to speak of and that Austin was full of all the kinds of people I didn't get along with: hippies, those heavily into vintage fashion, and people who cared about where their vegetables came from. Nah, I told everyone that I would rough it, live hard for a while, figure it out when I got there. My family and friends were gracious enough not to bring up how ridiculous this idea was, how I was not cut out for living hard. I mean, Christ, I'm the type of person who got stressed-out playing Monopoly. I'm not the hard-living type. So I was secretly a little relieved when I did the math and figured out my bank account couldn't support a plane ticket, or a moving van, or the amount of breakfast burritos I would no doubt consume there. So, back to the burbs it was.

Home, for me, is a suburban town in Westchester, New York. South Salem isn't quaint—I didn't know most of my neighbors' business and we didn't have some gentle town doctor who solved our maladies—it was just *typical*. These kinds of places have a reputation, and I can totally see why. It wasn't until I started watching TV shows set in the suburbs that I realized these portrayals were right.

Stereotypes of the Suburbs That Are Completely Correct

1. *There are a lot of white people.* I was the only Puerto Rican (well, half) in a sea of people who were excited to tell you about their European heritage. Since I had a bit of ethnic blood in me, my history teachers would always ask me my "feelings" about parts of history they thought I might be

invested in. ("And, Alida—what did *you* feel when you read about the Spanish-American War?" "Uh, bored? I'm not from Spain.") Besides using ancestry Web sites to discover they were vaguely related to Charles Lindbergh, white people in the burbs love expensive Mexican restaurants, new issues of the *Wall Street Journal*, and hiring ethnic ladies to take care of their kids.

2. *Yes, there are a lot of nannies.* My mom is all ethnic all of the time, and even *she* ended up taking care of some ginger kid for a couple of hours after her shifts at the dental office. When she married my super-white dad, people asked her how she handled a "mixed relationship." She stared at them, pretending not to know English, because honestly, fuck them.

3. *They care about stupid white-people problems.* The two biggest controversies of my hometown to date are (1) installing a cell-phone tower because service was terrible. People were worried about the "radiation" but mostly about how ugly the tower might look, and (2) this one girl performed a piece from the *Vagina Monologues* in our high school and got suspended because she (obviously) said the word *vagina* during it. In suburbia, there are no vaginas, only Cape Cod summer houses.

4. *People care about where their kids go to college way too*

much. Every WASP person who I went to high school with took thirty-five SAT prep courses to appease their polo-shirt-wearing-and-boutique-shopping parents. Ironically, a broad cross-section of these kids were the same ones who I witnessed chug gallons of milk in the parking lot of our high school. I don't know how many SAT courses would help that sort of idiocy.

5. *Malls are a thing.* What do you want to do this weekend, Katherine? Do you want to wander around and stare at monogrammed candles for three hours? You want a cinnamon pretzel? There you go, let's just hang out and take sexy MySpace pictures with a bunch of headless mannequins. We'll call it a Friday.

6. *"Responsible" parenting means being upstairs while they let their high school kids drink booze in their basement.* At half of the parties I ever went to, the mom was right upstairs, reading the new Crate and Barrel catalog and reasoning that if she knew her kids were drinking the beer she bought downstairs, they wouldn't go get it on their own. This reasoning, of course, is idiotic, but she still put her lavender body lotion on at night and fell asleep to the gentle aroma of being a good mother.

7. *A lot of kids were on Ritalin.* Hey! I think my kid is coloring too much! And he's not at the tippy-

top of his fourth-grade class! Let's drug him so much he is a robot! My brother's guidance counselor told my mother that because he wasn't "entirely into school," he should be pumped up with prescription medication. My mom refused to do it, because he clearly didn't have ADD. He now has a great job and a clear brain. That cannot be said about some of the other Ritalin-addled kids I grew up with.

8. *Everybody drives like a complete asshole.* They have expensive cars and bumper stickers declaring where their kid goes to college and who they voted for. And they do not signal when they are changing lanes.

As much as I like to rag on the suburbs, I had a perfectly idyllic childhood. There were swing sets and puppies and the kind of high school education where I had a guidance counselor who remembered my name. I just didn't get why I was *back*. At eighteen, I had packed up my two suitcases and a couple of boxes, and promised myself I would be "puttin' this whole fuckin' town in my rearview" (Ben Affleck, *The Town*). Though there was nothing specifically wrong with my family or my home, I had created a life plan that involved "city living at twenty-one till I have to come home and do my laundry for the weekend." Yet here I was, four years later, lugging those suitcases and the boxes back up to my childhood bedroom.

There are plenty of good things that happen when you move back to the place you grew up in, and those things last as long as you consider your move back to be *a vacation.* There were some luxurious accommodations in Hotel Nugent, and that included central air, a couch that didn't have crumbs on it, and my parents—who, unlike most people, thought I was interesting and cute. And the fridge, the glorious fridge! I'd never been able to maintain a fridge that didn't really act just like a pit that things would eventually rot in. My mother, however, didn't just have a fridge, she kept a *stocked fuckin' fridge.* There is nothing quite like the joy of opening it up to reveal three kinds of cheese, two kinds of hummus, various mustards, and leftover mashed potatoes I could nosh on in the middle of the night. There was fresh produce that wasn't limp and dead! There was juice and soda and milk! I couldn't believe my four eyes!

Also, we had an actual *liquor cabinet.* To this day, I do not have a liquor cabinet because a liquor cabinet is also known as a half a bottle of vodka that I keep in my freezer. My parents had Amaretto! They had *two different kinds of gin.* I was in heaven. Of course, you have to be careful drinking in front of your parents, but after a couple of weeks of living at home, I mastered the art of it.

HOW TO DRINK IN FRONT OF YOUR PARENTS

- At dinner, pour yourself a glass of wine. Then, when they turn around, guzzle that wine down and swiftly pour another. Pretend that never happened. Repeat.

- While watching television, loudly announce to your parents you need some juice. Say juice anywhere between three and four hundred times. Go to the fridge and pour some juice, and then add some liquor to it. Watch while your parents find amusement in your raucous laughter at *The King of Queens*. That Kevin James is just a riot! Why is his wife so mean?

- When your parents are sleeping, dreaming of sugar plums and the nonalcoholic child they once had, open the liquor cabinet like you are in high school again. Quietly. Carefully. Get drunk and watch HBO until it's 3 A.M.

- Any function attended by more than five relatives from your extended family is a green light to get shockingly drunk. They will understand. Family *makes* you drink.

And there were presents to be had, in the form of my own stuff that I rediscovered. Every time I opened up a drawer in my room, I was transported back to 2002, a relatively good year for capri pants, boy bands, and bangs. My room was a DeLorean time portal back to the old days. Coming across Britney Spears CDs in my drawer? You can't even imagine how fast I downloaded that shit on to my computer and began jamming out to "Lucky." She's a star! But she's tortured! It's like Britney knew about the *Real Housewives* before they even knew about themselves! The CDs were lying next to the various pictures I had taken at assorted bat mitzvahs and sweet sixteens. I remembered what love was like in the time of braces and was supremely glad I had stopped wearing three-quarter-knit Old Navy performance fleeces everywhere.

Eventually, though, the novelty of these things started to wear off. If anything, being around my old journals, riddled with dreams of both middle school boys and larger, worldly dreams, made me feel stagnant. *Here*, I was not living my dreams. It also didn't help that I was completely surrounded by pictures of myself as a child, a constant reminder of my arrested development. In fact, there are only two pictures that are prominent in my home from my college years—one of them was of me and my brother at my graduation, mid-ironic fist pump, the other of us at my cousin's wedding, grinning widely because we could see the open bar. The rest of the photos were of me in all sorts of stages of my life, laid out like photos for somebody's wake. Here I am being a two-year-old little shit sitting in a plastic pool. There I am at six—what you can't see in this school photo is my hairy legs (PS, If I ever have a little girl, I'm going to make her wax her mustache at eight. Poor me looked like a prepubescent boy till I was eleven). Here's me as a fourteen-year-old, posing with my grandmother by a Christmas tree, excited to wear a training bra for the holidays. (News flash: not real breasts, just baby fat.) Oh yeah, and right among them was my college degree my mother got framed and hung up over my old PC. The very PC where I played *The Sims* when I was a kid just so I could force the couples to make out (usually two guys). Right by the CD player that I listened to Kelly Clarkson on when I was sad about some guy whose name I can't even remember. All of these were little reminders that hey, you were a person on a path to dreams and success, which definitely did not include living at home again.

Being at home was like a mattress to fall back on with the smallest of peas on the bottom, just large enough to bother the princess. I was damn lucky that I had a place to call home, but I didn't like the feeling of stealing my parents food and being unable to tell them when I could ever afford my own. There were a lot of mixed signals about how I could be both Alida the child and Alida the adult. The weirdest thing about being home was living under the roof of the people who grew up telling me what to do yet being totally confused about what limits I now had. I was technically allowed to leave the house until all hours of the night, to go out drinking and not eat breakfast if I didn't want to, to sit close to the television and not clean my room, but I felt bizarre doing these things brazenly. It was a strange tug-of-war of expecta-tions. My folks tried to shut their mouth about my weird habits and respect my newfound quirks; meanwhile, I was looking for structure and comfort and familiarity in a time in my life where I had almost none. I *wanted* to have them tell me to get my ass into gear. To eat more protein. To cut back on the gin.

They didn't budge, though. And neither did I. My suitcases remained unpacked. *This is only temporary*, I kept telling myself, a mantra for a girl who didn't know when she would take her next steps.

Stalking was how I spent a large portion of my time at home. There wasn't a moment I didn't have my computer balanced on my lap, telling my friends how "this town is sooo lame, I just want to go to NYC and get drunk." I found old classmates online who moved back home and tried to gauge what they were doing without making any contact with them. Some were stagnant. Some of them went to grad school, those lucky procrastinators. Some wrote about commuting, which meant they already had jobs and I wanted to drown them. Some lived in expensive apartments in expensive cities, and I knew, just knew, that their parents were paying for them. Nobody seemed to be doing *that great*, but most of them lied about it pretty well. Nobody wants to say, "I'm trying to get my feet on the ground" when they're in their twenties. They want you to think they're about to do something dangerous, or exciting, or different. We're not "living at home," we're "crashing until we can afford a pad in Brooklyn."

And I was the worst offender. I was *too good* for this. Being among all of my old CDs and clothes and journals was apparently turning me into a teenager again—but this time, the mean girl who I never even *was* in high school, the kind of girl who wore a lot of eyeliner and painted her middle finger in black sharpie and had sex TOO SOON. All exasperated sighs and eye rolls, like nobody but the people on the Internet could ever understand me. I snapped at my parents over ridiculous things: *Mom, this isn't the right kind of hummus, it's not even creamy.* I constantly bitched to my friends about how there were no good bars, good restaurants, good people, good *anything* about being home.

The few times I summoned the courage and motivation to go out, it was to the kind of bars where only Top 40 music was played and greasy Italian-American men fist-pumped through the crowd. I'd sip on my whiskey indifferently, biding my time patiently with my brother and his friends. And inevitably, I wouldn't even finish my first drink when somebody would scream "ALIDA?!?!?!?!" with the enthusiasm only novelty and alcohol could produce.

Whoosh. They would descend on me—girls who used to have the same crushes as me and wear similar Tiffany bracelets who were now paralegals, social workers, in nursing school. Real jobs. My old classmates who I hadn't seen in years, and who I thought I'd never see again. They would hug and paw at me and I would struggle to answer their questions. *No, I haven't seen her in a while. Ha, yeah, I was in Boston. I was going to move to Austin. Yeah, in Texas. But yeah, I'm gonna move to New York soon. No, I'm here for only a little bit longer. I haven't even unpacked, seriously.* Every word out of my mouth was a little bit bitter, each sip of my drink empowering me to act higher and mightier, when deep down, I was just awkward and uncomfortable. I wanted these girls to realize *I was going to do something with my life*, and not stay here forever. They listened to me, until they saw somebody more interesting—an old football jock from my high school who was supposedly doing very well in the "real estate game," a girl who was fifteenth runner-up on *American Idol*. It was clear we had nothing in common anymore, but I would squeal appropriately, promise to keep in touch, and then retreat home in misery. A nerd turned a mean girl turning into a loner.

Three months and forty thousand job applications later, I was still a permanent resident of my parents' house. Still annoyed, still stubborn, still living out of suitcases like I was moving out any day now. But reality and fate were destined to smack me in the face. It came, as most things do in my life, via television.

It started off innocently enough. I was with my family watching television, and my parents let me have the remote because they are nice. I tried to put on something that I thought we could "all enjoy" because my dad thinks HBO is stupid, my mom doesn't like *It's Always Sunny in Philadelphia* because Danny DeVito unnerves her, and I would watch anything but cage fighting. I found something about women who almost perfectly murder their husbands, opened a beer, and we were all very happy.

When it went to commercial break, however, things got a little uncomfortable. Those stupid back-to-school commercials kept coming on, the ones where the kids are dancing around and gleefully sharpening pencils and happily making sandwiches for their brown-bag lunches. Seeing those commercials about "the most wonderful time of year" used to piss me off when I was in high school, but now? It felt *really* awkward, kind of like sitting with your parents during a sex scene in a movie. The school supplies were a gloomy reminder: "Hey, lady, now it's September and you're doing . . . what?" Not getting ready for science, not getting ready for teacher's dirty looks . . . also not getting ready for any semblance of a career, so it seemed.

After seeing a few painful rounds of these commercials, my dad turned to me and said, "Alida, since you're not going to be headin' back to school anytime soon, maybe you should do something else productive. Like *unpack your stuff*." It was a joke that fell flat because the audience didn't want to hear it.

It was confirmed. They didn't think it was a pit stop. There were no job offers rolling in, and I was wearing the same clothes days in a row. It was time to face the music—I was going to have to sit and stay for a while.

As much as I hated hearing it, this was the push I needed. This wasn't winter break between semesters. This wasn't just "hanging out with the parental units." It felt like a punch to the gut, but a necessary one. I started to protest but stopped. Who was I? My whole "figuring out my future" was being stalled by my inability to act like an adult. An adult recognizes circumstances. An adult *unpacks her suitcase*. With wounded pride, I headed upstairs, ready to face the task before me. Out came the college notebooks with the little doodles on them, the ornamental shot glasses, the papers on Jane Austen, the leftover pieces of a life I no longer lived.

An hour or so later, my mom came into my room and sat on my bed, eyeing the piles that I had now strewn across the floor. I could tell she wanted to say something about *how* I was unpacking, but she was biting her tongue. She instead sat quietly, surveying the questionable wardrobe choices of her adult daughter, which were now fully on display. My mom, bless her, is always concerned that I am ruining my "pretty face and adorable figure" with the things I choose to do to it. I can't say she's wrong. Some days, I'll slap on a skirt, a nice blazer, and wear a cute but fashion-forward button-down, but then the next, I'll put on baggy denim shorts and my favorite cutoff top, a bright orange thing that says "Jump for JESUS," with little sneakers on it. I caught the pained look on her face when I pulled out a weird fuzzy vest I had thought would make me look like an LA girl in a band. (I didn't. I looked like a third grader who dressed herself like a Build-A-Bear.) A ripped tie-dyed crop top looked like it was going to put her over the edge.

Glancing at my mom's face, I started to get an idea of what she was thinking during these last few months: *Okay, my daughter is cutting off all her hair and wearing dumb shit and staying up till 4 A.M. on the Internet. She seems to like wine a lot. Should I be concerned? She's still the same sarcastic little wiseass I know, but is she going insane? Is she applying for enough jobs? The right ones? Should I say something?*

My mom and I have always been close. She's always asked

me about my problems, and because she did, I told her about them. She always knew who I was dating, who I had a crush on, what friend was pissing me off, and how I was afraid of dying alone or gaining one thousand pounds so I'd have to be wheeled out of the house by paramedics for a one-hour TV special. She was fine with everything I did and respected the choices I made. But it must have been a little odd for her, seeing how her daughter actually *lived*. Not just what I told her on the phone, but she got to *see it, every day, and in her face.* My parents had loved me and raised me, sent me on my way for a few years, and now I had come back a slightly different person. They hadn't known of my habit of speaking out of the side of my mouth. They didn't realize that I had become twice as socially anxious or that I liked artichokes now. Little things, but things that started to compose Alida: The Adult Years.

And at the same time, I wanted to prove that I was somebody who could rank with them, or at least somebody who could *be* something. That's why I was fighting unpacking. I didn't want to disappoint them, deep down, and I didn't want to disappoint myself.

Somewhere around there, I think my mother realized that she was done raising me. I wasn't a kid anymore, even if my version of "adult" wasn't exactly working seamlessly. Now she only had to give me advice, hug me, remind me that I needed to take vitamins, and tell me that I looked pretty with my hair longer. I could choose to take that advice, or I couldn't, but it wasn't up to my parents to get me anywhere anymore. We both let the high school Alida who lived in this house go.

"Thanks, Mom," I said to her, for no real reason she could latch on to.

"Do you want me to make dinner for you? You, uh . . . bought groceries, right?" My privilege was showing, a badge of something that looked a little bit like lucky.

I unpacked slowly that night, putting all the things I had collected in college in the old, familiar drawers. My new life finally connected with my old life.

Months later, with the help from freelance jobs, part-time gigs, and prayers to Satan, I would scrounge enough money to move out. All things change, and if you want them enough, they change faster than you expect. Money was saved, plans were made, and before I knew it, I stood in my childhood bedroom with the Britney Spears CDs and closed the door to move somewhere else. Suburban life with my parents hadn't stilted my growth; in reality, it had taught me that some things, if you were lucky enough, would always be there if you needed them.

"Should I start taking these posters down?" my mother asked me, always looking for a new home project to take on.

"No, Mom, leave them. Just in case."

Get a Job, You Bum

After I graduated college and was on month six of joblessness, I kept encountering people who asked me how I was "dealing with being unemployed," with the same tone people use to ask "Are you okay?" after someone dies. Scrunched face, head tilted to the side, cautious concern in their voice. Relatives, neighbors, former classmates who wanted to secretly gloat about their sweet job at NBC—it didn't matter who, but inevitably, the first question out of their mouths involved why I didn't have a job yet. The reason was because I got a degree in pipe dreams and graduated into a festering hell pit of a terrible economy, but you know. I was dealing with it just fine, thanks for asking, just keeping on keeping on, applying for anything and everything, and ha-ha, yeah, it was nice to have some spare time! Truth was, though, the freedom of "doing whatever I want, whenever I want, and doing it while pantsless" was becoming miserable for me. I had kept a steady job since I was sixteen years old. While the first weeks of nothing to do were filled with "I can get up *whenever*" glee, that loses its luster pretty damn fast.

What does one do when every day is an open-ended schedule? Let's see. I ate a lot. I organized my clothes by color one day. I tried to cut my own hair. Mostly, I did a *lot* of lazing around. I tried to get up early in the morning, because every time I got up after 12 P.M., I felt like I was acting like the irresponsible stepfather of my own life. Because I had little else to do those mornings other than the suffocating and immense task of finding a job, I often spent my time watching hours of morning TV. Here's my theory about early-morning shows: They're annoying and terrible on purpose to encourage people to get off the couch and get a job. I had always known there were a significant number of people in this country who did not know the identity of their fathers, but until my stint of unemployment, I didn't realize the verifiable insanity of those who choose to go on television to discuss this topic. These shows are filled with screaming women with heaving breasts who managed to sleep with the skinniest, slimiest men without teeth they could find. Then they'd cut to this adorable baby who was probably thinking "Well, either way I think I'm pretty much screwed with *whoever* my parents are, so I better start saving for college now." All of the commercials were basic variations of *CALL THIS NUMBER AND GO BACK TO SCHOOL. FOR CHRIST'S SAKE, WHY ARE YOU WATCHING THIS?!* Watching trashy morning shows day after day was pretty much the only inspiration I had to become employed again.

But no matter how much Maury inspired me to get my ass off the couch and Monster.com it up for hours on end, I had to face reality. I had graduated with a liberal arts degree from a small, artsy school, and therefore my marketable skills were limited to talking about queer theory and knowing how to wear clothes from Goodwill to look like an Olsen twin. My résumé pretty much looked this:

Alida A. Nugent

Here's my e-mail address and my phone number.

It's funny that I put these here because you're not going to call me, are you?

EDUCATION

Emerson College, Bachelor of Arts in "Writing"
May 2010

I put that "writing" part in quotes because I know what you're already thinking—that it wasn't the best choice for a career path and that I'm probably not very good with math. I'm terrible at math, so you're right about that. Dude, it's not like I'm going to ask you to read my stories, okay? I'm just going to work your shitty little job filing papers and doing blurbs about movies or maybe correcting a memo that has some typos every once in a while. You should just be happy that I have a basic understanding of word processing programs, which I am now representing poorly in this not-very-well-formatted résumé.

Was on the Dean's List once.

And academic probation twice, maybe three times.

EXPERIENCE

This One Comedy Troupe

Because that's a real fucking "skill," huh? Writing three-minute sketches about businessmen in space and performing them to a bunch of bored, drunk underclassmen? But I was treasurer! I always handed the forms in late; oh god, please don't judge me.

This One Writing Piece I Did

For a literary magazine that I will lie about and say I edited content in for three years, which I didn't, but I assume I would have done a decent job if I had.

Coffee Shop Job

My experience should prove to you that I am only qualified to work in another coffee shop, but I'm going to go for the gold anyway. Did you know that I was late for work a lot? If you hire me, that's your cross to bear. However, I did fairly well on my biyearly reviews with praise like, "Doesn't yell at people as much or look nearly as miserable as she did a year ago."

PROFICIENT IN

At least one of the eight computer programs I have just listed. Oh, and I'm really good with people. But only if I'm drinking with them.

With this stacked résumé, it's a shock that I didn't get hired right away as an editor for a prestigious magazine, or as a features writer for a totally cool music Web site, or at least, as a homeless prop comic.

It wasn't completely my fault that I wasn't having any luck. The economy had bottomed out and the job market, at this point, seemed to be 80 percent "knowing people." And I didn't know anybody at all. I never *tried* to get to know people, because I didn't want the terrible reputation of being a networker when I was still in college. You know who I'm talking about: the douchebag who bought business cards online that said "entrepreneur" on them when they were *still in school*. I might not have had a lot of motivation in college but my sole one may have been to not be *that* guy at the party. I couldn't be that person even if I wanted to, though, because my networking skills are comparable to that of a rabid pit bull let loose in a nursery school. I hate being persistent, I don't like wearing sweaters to "functions," and I never want to attempt putting my entire body up somebody else's ass. My brother told me that with my people skills and tendency toward being grubby, I might do well as a garbageman, a job that had better benefits and more pay than any position I'd hold in the next ten years. I was disappointed to find out that even for *that* job you need a goddamn connection. Hopeless. Even the simplest positions, the mindless ones where all you had to do was file and put stuff in alphabetical order and say hello into a phone, were as competitive as going after an Olympic gold medal. To have your résumé considered, an applicant needed approximately sixteen years of secretarial school and also must be able to manage wrangling in a pack of wolves while bedazzling a jacket. You must also be a wizard, Harry.

Since full-time jobs that were attractive and relevant to my education didn't seem to exist, I started to apply for every other job under the sun, including the part-time ones and the dreaded internships. Part-time jobs were limited: coffee shops, sex workers, bartenders. I couldn't be a bartender because becoming a bartender in New York City required bigger breasts than I had, unending patience, and the blood of a first born. But I figured I could probably land an internship. You know, because I needed more "experience" to do something that I was trained to do in college.

Application after application went out, and day after day I'd hear nothing. I was getting fed up. So eventually I did what I do when I get fed up: drink. Not that this really makes my case any better, but in order to ease my frustrations, I started to apply to internships while drinking (sorry, Mom). I would curl up on my couch at eleven at night, clutching my glass of wine like I was about to send a text to a guy I had a crush on, and you know how that goes. Panic eases with one glass of wine, one turns into five, and soon enough, applying for internships and shit jobs seemed almost *entertaining*.

I was never good at cover letters when I was sober, because I felt like I was selling myself for something I didn't even want in the first place, so writing them with a belly full of wine? They weren't my most shining of moments:

Example One

To Whom It May Concern:

Twenty minutes ago, I changed from my track shorts to my "goin' out shorts," which are, in fact, just long denim shorts that I find acceptably cool because they are ripped. Why am I telling you this? Because this is my life now, posteducation. This is the bed I am laying in or lying in. I'm not even sure how to use that correctly anymore, although in case you are wondering, I am quite dignified enough to write this note sitting up.

But, in all honesty, you should hire me in my postgraduate state because I am an ambitious person who promises to work extremely hard for very little money. I make very good coffee, and I have been told my fax sending is unparalleled. I also understand the concepts of "coming to work on time" and "being relatively quiet." I have worked hard for four years at an urban writing program, so one day I can begin work at an entry-level job so I can one day be paid for being funny. I believe that a company such as yours would be an honor and a privilege to work for—I would love to do whatever I can to start my career with you.

Sincerely yours,
Alida Nugent

This went to a comedy Web site directed toward girls, and not only did I tell them I didn't know the correct usage of the word *lay*, I also think that the phrase *whatever I can* has the connotation that I would sleep with anybody who would hire me at this point. (There is no way I would get hired for my sexual skills. I drool too much during oral.)

Example Two

Hello. My name is Alida Nugent. I'm a 22-year-old recent college grad who enjoys watching Intervention *and is disturbed by Eminem's comeback. I want to make money writing funny things or at least encounter a magical world where loans are in the past and I don't have to work a service job anymore. I read [the Web site] because it makes me laugh and I like knowing that some people's first time with sex was worse than mine. I have this fantasy where you let me write for you for three months for no pay and I make you good coffee (I used to work as a barista—six years) and you hire me because I am so funny and then Jesus comes back and fixes everything. OH.*

Okay, so I guess this blurb is supposed to sound professional. Well, I can be professional, too. I wear button-down shirts and I know what "come to work on time" means. I have a great phone voice. I make copies with the best of them.

Sincerely,
Alida Nugent

This one was for a pop-culture Web site, and a relatively popular one at that. I imagine that, at the time, I thought the Jesus reference was adorable. It is probably becoming alarmingly clear to you that I have little to no sense of professionalism.

The urgency to find a job came along with my first loan bill. With a snap of the fingers, the days of drunk applications and hangin' on the couch watching *Maury* were over. I opened up the stark white envelope with trepidation, and there the letter was, asking me kindly to pay up:

Hello, Alida!

If you can believe it, your six months since graduation are now up. I'm going to ask you to stop screaming now. Hope this finds you happy, and by happy I mean you have lots of money in your pocket, because now you have to start paying us back about twice as much as you borrowed. It's not a big deal, just around three hundred dollars every month till you turn thirty-eight years old. If you don't do that, we'll ruin your credit and you'll never be able to buy a car or an apartment or happiness, because you can now buy happiness. That was a little joke, but it wasn't, because if you don't pay us back we will find you. When you are sleeping. And we will steal your childhood blankie or saw off one of your arms. We'll then steal your first-born child from the floating-child heaven sky, or hire a spirit stealer to ruin your life. For example: Every

uplifting movie that you watch about animals from now
on will end in tragedy. It will be very sad, or "ruff"
(another joke).

Love, Loans

My first check was sent with bitterness, marking a cold, hard day in my life. ADULTHOOD was officially here, and I needed to get off my ass and embrace it. It was more motivating than the makeover montage in *Clueless,* or for you old-timers, a *Rocky* montage. I had to step up my game and put this diploma to good use, or else the mustachioed loan guys would come after me.

When you go to college and expect your career to take off like the *Rocketeer,* and the only options that you have in front of you are not even mildly related to what you studied, you will become a little desperate to work anywhere. Despite being from a liberal arts background, I didn't really have a strong opinion about "being a corporate drone," which is something a character would say on a show where they generalize art kids. I had no problem being a corporate drone if it paid my bills and thereby tried to get a job doing secretarial work in an office. I had done it before, on break from college during the summer, and let me tell you, it was not as charming and cute as Pam Halpert makes it seem.

Number one rule of working a secretarial job: You should probably be okay with answering a phone. Even now, the sound of a landline phone makes me pee my pants a bit, because I think it's somebody older than me calling to yell at me. When most people call an office, they are under the impression that whoever answered the phones knows absolutely *everything* about the company they are calling. And I never knew the answers. "Do you know when my case will be reviewed?" a guy would frantically yell on the other end of the receiver. *Um, sorry, no, I don't*, I would answer. When people caught on to that, their rage grew tie-wearing wings. *Why NOT?* Uh, because I am wearing a blazer I got from the junior's section of your local department store, that's why. I am young enough to be your grandchild, and I spent the twenty minutes before you called me reading about how Sarah Michelle Gellar's baby daughter eats sushi.

Number two rule of being a decent secretary: Master the art of filing. One would assume this seems like an easy task as long as you know the alphabet. Well, imagine the library the Beast presents to Belle. That's a real nice library, right? Now imagine having to put everything in that humongous library in order, except thirty people have the same name, forty million of the files you need to put away have gone missing, and it's eight in the morning. The Disney magic fades mighty fast, you best believe it.

After a few weeks of working at an office, I realized I was becoming the kind of person who was finding joy in the little things—and by little things, I mean meaningless, stupid distractions from my shitty job. A reprieve of going to the copy machine and getting the pleasure of mindlessly staring at the wall for five minutes was magical. Trips to the bathroom were a joyous urination break where I washed my hands till they became pruney. And don't forget about the absolute thrill of lunch. I couldn't wait to run to the freezer and get out my little prepackaged frozen dinner, a low-calorie macaroni and cheese that I would eat with the same delight a child experiences on Christmas morning. On the occasions that I went out beyond the office doors to buy a salad, you'd think I was being let out of prison after a twenty-year sentence. I was becoming weak, mostly due to the large consumption of Lean Cuisine, and the only way I could fight da power was to dye a huge bloodred streak in my hair that made me look like an anime character. This, I suspect, was why they eventually told me they "didn't need me anymore." Nobody wants to be greeted by a sad little girl with terrible hair who spends most of her time making PowerPoint projects of dinosaurs eating chimpanzees. I realized I could and would not be able to hold another secretarial job again. We were as incompatible as people who are normal and people who think it's normal to speed date.

Thus I entered the world of freelance work, something I heartily recommend to any depressed liberal arts graduate. When I decided to enter the world of freelance writing, I let out a large sigh, which is good, because freelance jobs are the exhausted sigh of the job world. It's giving up without really giving up. There *are* freelancers who get paid a lot and are their own boss and love it. That takes years and motivation and patience, and is very admirable. Mostly, though, young freelancers are people who realize they are unemployable and therefore need to do something to pay their bills, even if it means you get treated like shit. It's the easiest job to land because you don't get any health care benefits, or a steady pay, or any emotional security. It's sort of like working for Aunt March in *Little Women* or your fourth-grade teacher who hated you. You are hired under the premise that they are not expected to care about you at all, but they have decided to take on the burden of looking after you anyway.

My first job was to write lots of lists about pop culture, spending hours scouring the Internet for more than six vampires I would have sex with. The bosses would send thousands of passive-aggressive e-mails with "Do you THINK YOU CAN HANDLE this workload?" even though it was a 750-word assignment. I would reply equally as passive-aggressively with a "maybe ☺." I never met any of these people I wrote for, and I used to imagine them all as Emily Blunt in *The Devil Wears Prada*, but perhaps with a chic pair of pants from the Loft.

After a while, I acquired three freelance jobs for three different Web sites, and I found myself miserably terrible at all of them. Every article I posted was greeted with nightmarish responses from various men taking breaks from masturbating on Chatroulette to troll the Internet. "This girl can't write for shit," they would start, and this would lead to the eventual sort of conclusion about how I should be killed for my writing. You'd be surprised how many people took the time to discuss how I needed to be murdered for my scathing opinion on sexy television cops. It was very encouraging.

From a business angle, I was even worse off. In freelance,

they don't pay you unless you send in an invoice. I am incredibly bad at paperwork, because it takes only four minutes to complete but feels like such a large task. A simple spreadsheet was too much for *this* naïve college grad! I would often forget to send in invoices or keep track of the jobs I did, and would therefore not get paid. You also don't get taxed while working freelance—they let you tax yourself, mostly because they don't believe you're a real citizen of America yet. Idiotic me spent all my money and didn't actually think about taxes until April, until I owed almost three thousand dollars to the government because I wasted a year of my life making silly jokes about Rihanna. For a job that doesn't believe you can handle a full-time responsibility, they certainly give you a lot of responsibilities. I was bad at all of them.

The worst part about the job, I think, was that it made me realize how much I wanted to be paid to be a writer. I would wake up at noon, burping old whiskey, sit down in front of my on-its-last-legs laptop, and write for a couple of hours about things I hated. I loved it, though, not because of what I was doing at the moment but because of what I might be able to eventually *do* with this experience. I loved the feeling of getting a paycheck by people who didn't care about me, to write for people who wanted my head chopped off. It felt dirty and gross and thrilling.

"Ah," I said. "I'm getting paid peanuts and am relatively pleased with myself. I'd like to find more ways to do this, for more money, and probably for the rest of my life."

Sitting in my pajamas, seeing if my seventy-five dollars had gone through to my checking account, I realized what I wanted. It wasn't a *where*, it was a *where to next*, small steps toward my eventual goal of becoming a full-time writer. This was my start.

This is the one perk to being young and underemployed—you find a trajectory for your daydreams, of getting more or wanting more or wanting something different. And when you're working toward your dreams, you have to start at the bottom. The idea that we should all start at the low end of the totem pole is the kind of sentiment that has been passed on to our generation from all the ones before it, but it's still good advice. Toughing it out is essential no matter what year we were born, and it probably won't get any easier anytime soon. You've got to be willing to do a lot of thankless things before you see any reward. Taking shit is how you get up to the top; working hard is how you stay for years at the bottom until you move up slowly to middle ground.

It's daunting to go after the things you want, even when you're not entirely sure they will always be the things you want. I'll tell you, however, what you do want—a fire under your ass. A push. A constant toward something better. This is something I'm willing to suffer for, 750 words at a time.

Save a Five, Lose a Hundred

'm not good at saving money, probably because I don't have a lot of it. If I took all the money I had out of my bank account and recklessly spent it, I could relax for one day in a soup kitchen by a Sandals resort, staring wistfully at the family-filled water. I could pay a lady to let me hold Gucci. I could fly economy class to Vegas and double my money, then lose it, then sadly kiss a bathroom attendant until he brings me an alcoholic slushie the size of my head. The older I get, though, the more I feel pressure to actually use my savings account for savings, rather than spending the little money I have on iced coffee and $4.99 Julia Roberts DVDs.

So one day, with a bottle of two-dollar wine and my "accounting hat" on (which is an optimistic but clinically depressed fedora), I wrote out a budget. I am sharing it here because I assume we have a lot in common, like money woes and destructive behavior. The next few pages contain a list of my monthly required expenses, followed by ways I have saved money. You can copy it and adjust the numbers as you see fit.

Monthly Expenses

Place of residence: Home is where the largest chunk of your cash goes! For some, it's an apartment or house. For others, it's free because you live with your parents, which is a smart saving technique if you're okay having to pay via long-winded conversations with your parents about how Twitter works, how you are aware that it is stupid, and how the phrase *going steady* does not exist anymore. For me, it's a decrepit shoe box apartment that houses an assortment of rodents and critters. **Cost: eight hundred dollars a month to a man I have seen only once.**

Electric and gas and phone and cable bills, oh my!: Cable is required for me, and so is the Internet, because I am obviously chained to both. Why watch TV if you can't look at .gifs from the NBC Thursday lineup even though you already watched it and remember what happened? So those bills are handled swiftly, like my life depends on it. Electric bills, though, don't need to be handled so vigilantly—maybe once every four months, until a notice comes in the mail that the company is going to turn it off. This gives me the incentive to pay it, but it comes with two hours of waiting on hold, listening to an upbeat voice recording of how to reduce your energy bill by not being such a baby about the heat, which maybe isn't worth the delay. **Cost: 350 dollars, if I choose to bite the bullet, dig through my e-mails to find the account number, and pay it.**

Toiletries: Inevitably, my roommates will eventually hint to the fact that I have not been the one to buy toilet paper in months but let me off the hook because they know I don't *mean* to be such a bad roommate. So in order to hold on to the few friends I still have, I go to the local Duane Reade drugstore and stock up on toilet paper, which is reasonably priced when purchased in bulk, for around eleven dollars. Then I decide I need to try dark lipstick because my makeup routine is getting predictable. Passing through to the cosmetics aisle, I decide my hair could use more volume and say to myself, "This twelve-dollar hairspray should do the trick." And ooh ... sweet 'n salty Chex Mix. And bodywash that smells like coconuts! And cleaning products that look fun and might encourage me to actually clean! **Cost: forty-five dollars, if I'm lucky.**

Laundry: Sure, I could do laundry myself for mere quarters, but I do not know where my drier sheets are, and my towel smells like mold and I do not know the steps to get rid of it, so I just avoid the task as long as possible. **Cost: twelve dollars to the laundry service when I finally decide to do it. It may not be a lot in the long run, but it's an exorbitant amount to spend on eight-dollar shirts I could've washed myself.**

Food: Groceries are never required. Required trips to the beloved snack warehouse Trader Joe's are. Sure, I forget to buy sensible things, like eggs, and avoid purchasing marinara sauce because it's too heavy to carry, but I'll stock up on frozen pasta dishes that cost more than it would to make it myself, buckets of hummus, blocks of brie for four dollars, and five different things that are "artisanal" because they're coated in chocolate or Tuscan herbs. And, inevitably, the wait on the never-ending line tires me out, so I end up calling all my friends to see which one of them will eat Thai food out with me, spending double the amount I saved. Brunch is a weekend necessity. Late-night pizza is essential, too, because nothing will humble you more than eating a lukewarm slice at 2 A.M., letting the sauce dribble down your shameful body. **Cost: probably hundreds, I'm too afraid to add it up. God help us all if there are birthday dinners this month held at cozy cafés that cost three dollars a bite.**

Credit card bill and college loans or "what is the possible minimum I can pay and how does it seem like every time I pay a dollar, another mountain owed appears?" **Cost: around 600 dollars, the ability to have a decent credit report, and little pieces of my soul.**

Clothing: One has to look nice. One has to cheer oneself up by going to a popular tween clothing superstore and purchasing clothing that are "real risk-taking pieces," like that one studded dress I've seen on high school girls on their fashion blogs. One will always need newer shoes. One will always feel better wearing a different outfit to the same bar with the same people. **Cost: If it's a season change, I drop at least 150 dollars. There's twelve seasons in a year, right?**

Drinking: How else would talking to people be fun? How else would kissing be so enjoyable? I'm not saying that my life is filled with despair, I'm just saying that if I stay sober for too long I start looking at life as a long day's journey into never getting out of debt and eventually being an old lady who thinks *Frasier* is funny. Gin is the way to my heart, or vodka, or wine after a long day, or shots to celebrate a great joke somebody just made about pop culture. Alcohol is everyone's friend, and I am always willing to shower my friend with lots of money. I'll include late-night cabs drunkenly navigating a cab driver who didn't want to take me home anyway in this category. **Cost: (Redacted for the sake of my mother's blood pressure).**

Unforeseen expenses: According to my horoscope, sometimes the unexpected can happen. Sometimes I need to buy *The Hurt Locker* on DVD so I can see Jeremy Renner's face. Sometimes I need to drop various technologies in the toilet. Or go to the movie theaters and give my liver a break. Buy a book to remind my brain there are other things out there besides computer screens. Finally get around to buying a garbage can for my room instead of scattering clothing tags around it like an Easter egg hunt. You only live once, says rappers and other people who don't believe in reincarnation. **Cost: more than you'd think! Like, almost a billion dollars!**

Total: A lot! I don't know, I'm on glass of wine number three and this is depressing.

Don't fret, though, because I have come up with some foolproof tips that will certainly help me save money and/or my sanity, though realistically, probably neither!

Tips for Saving

- Don't get an air conditioner, just hang out your window and have the neighborhood children chuck ice cubes at your face.
- Go on dates and make somebody spend money on you, because that is a thing that happens never, you romantic fool.
- Never go to the doctor! Who wants to know if you're sick? That's such a buzzkill. Medicate with sleep and misery and fear, instead!
- Instead of getting HBO, which costs maybe a million dollars a month, try to find episodes online. Worry the cops will come and shoot you for trying to catch the last episode of *Game of Thrones*; cry hysterically to your roommate until he gives you his HBO GO password.
- Talk about Twitter enough so that everybody hates you and nobody invites you out anymore.
- Save some money on razors by . . . BAHAHA, I know you've had the same razor for eighty-four years.
- Instead of eating out at fancy restaurants, eat a tablespoon of hummus, a handful of potato chips, a squirt of mustard, and maybe forty-six gummy vitamins while standing in your kitchen. Ask your roommates to serve you glasses of water that have food crust on them for the full experience.
- Don't get a manicure, bite your nails VERY CARE-FULLY.

- Go home for a weekend and stare at your mother with wide eyes until she buys you something for dinner and, if you're lucky, maybe a bra or some socks.
- Save money on bars by sitting alone in a dark living room, watching Food Network and dribbling wine on your chin. If you get wistful for the bar life, put on some heels, rub water (sweat!) all over yourself, play pop remixes very loudly, hold your pee in for an hour while "pretending to get home," and then fall and hate yourself.
- Marry somebody rich like all those hot guys who worked at Enron (THROWBACK).
- Guilt your friends into buying you drinks by saying you're depressed about a breakup you had thirty years ago.
- Go back in time before college, write the song "Call Me Maybe," and dive into your piles of money.
- Make your smartphone a stupid phone by turning off the Internet.
- Shave off half of your electric bill by going to bed at a reasonable hour instead of staying up till 3 A.M. to stare at cats and people you hate on Facebook.
- Blow up all the Forever 21s to avoid temptation.
- Sue a large corporation for charging you for guacamole on your burrito and totally become victorious like Erin Brockovich.
- Stop drinking coffee; just use good old-fashioned fear of the unknown to keep yourself awake.

- Purposefully get gently hit by a vehicle and let the government thank you for your bravery.
- Money doesn't buy you happiness! Do something for free, like going outside or sobbing or some other shit.
- Give up all your hobbies.
- The Countess says money doesn't buy you class, so cross your legs and watch Bravo until you speak in a Klonopin-like trance of faux British accents and Pilates and baked tilapia.
- Stop doing laundry; wear the same jeans forever and ever and ever.
- Don't go to the movies, just stare at Adam Sandler's new movie poster and hate everything.
- Sex is free BUT so is not having sex.
- Accidentally spend money! I NEVER SAID I WAS HELPFUL.

Savings: A reasonable amount, I'd say. At least a couple of dollars, if you're lucky. Don't go spending it on lottery tickets!

There you go, kids. I really feel like I have done my job here and been very helpful to you all. Look at what I did—I've taught you a hard truth about yourself and about the world. It will be years till you have significant money of any kind, and mere moments before you have to spend what little you do have. It's not pretty, but at least it's true. If you want to become truly free of monetary needs, do yourself a favor and free yourself of the chains of consumerism. Cancel your Facebook and go live in the woods for a while, run with the deer that care not what you wear or look like! That'll show the world! Or you could try to become fiscally responsible, like a weirdo nobody wants to listen speak because of how annoying and uppity you are. At best, you could get another credit card.

That'll work . . . until next month.

How to Romantically Destroy Yourself

Even though we were raised in the same household, my brother and I have entirely different views on love and romance. It's not a gender or age thing. It's that he simmers and I boil over. I explode with the idea of somebody—the friend of the friend whose wild hand gesticulations fill me with poetic sensibilities, the guy who works at the bar I frequent who remembers my name. My brother, on the other hand, is a pragmatist. He can date a lady for months without even thinking if he even wants to "you know, *actually*" date her. He can discount somebody for practical reasons: distance, religion, crazy parents.

I learned about the love line in the sand between the two of us when I was twenty-three, the year I binged on romcoms and poems by e.e. cummings, the year after I binged on zombie films and didn't think too much about matters of the heart. Twenty-three was the year I became a romantic. My brother, three years my elder, embraced twenty-six as the year he dated a lot and settled for anybody. I leaned toward guys who were better in my head than on paper. He leaned toward girls who were better-looking in person than in really great bikini pictures.

These are the kinds of polarizing differences you find out about your sibling when it's 3 P.M. on a Sunday and you're drinking beer and playing "Pro, Con, Deal-breaker, Neutral." The rules of the game are simple. You make up personality traits about a potential mate: "He talks to you in baby talk in public," "Ray Romano is her father," "He has a Roomba," or "She only watches Rob Zombie movies," and see how this affects your feelings about this imaginary person. It's a game that makes you realize more people are attracted to lazy eyes than you had previously thought.

My brother turned to me. "Okay, so what if the guy has sought out and murdered a guy who murdered his father? Would you date him then?"

My eyes lit up. This was *gold* to me. The action hero, the John Connor badass of my dreams.

"Are you *kidding me*??? That would be awesome! This is a superpro! This is a double triple pro! Sign me up for this dude if you know him."

My bro's eyebrows furrowed all the way down to his cheeks. He took a long sip of beer and looked at me with the kind of stare that means I was about to get a lecture. His eyes held the same concern as a father finding vodka in his high school daughter's desk in ABC family shows.

"Alida. *For Christ's sake.* Run away as fast as you can from that dude! He's got rage issues! He took the law into his own hands! He probably has post-traumatic stress disorder, a warrant for his arrest, and a really bad temper! What the hell is wrong with you? When are you going to learn? *Your life is not a MOVIE!*"

Of course my life is a movie, I wanted to tell him. I've been the heroine of my own personal action-movie-romantic-comedy hybrid for years! At the current time of filming, I just hadn't reached the good parts yet. I was stuck in the first twenty minutes—where the lead heroine wears glasses and dates a bunch of wrong guys and her life is the job. I hadn't bumped into the gruff man who I would hate, eventually fall for, discover he was a thief trying to steal my father's jewels, hate again, get saved by, then forgive and marry.

My brother continued on his rant, a rant he had been formulating, he said, since I brought home my second high school boyfriend, Calvin.

"That was when I thought to myself, *Oh boy. My baby sister has terrible taste in men.* Do you think I carried a baseball bat in my trunk because I played baseball? I didn't. I don't. I had to keep you away from the kinds of guys who hang outside the deli, trying to buy beer. I bet you had a crush on every single one of them."

"No," I corrected him. "The man of my dreams in high school was the kind of guy who lived on the wrong side of the tracks, the side that had bodegas that didn't card. Besides, J, when I was seventeen, I was dating that twenty-two-year-old. He could buy beer on any track side!"

He ignored my winning points and continued, ordering

more beer for energy. I needed a guy who paid for dinner on the first date. I needed a guy who called me consistently, who was there for me and did thoughtful things for me and other people. I needed somebody *nice*, he said, because I was nice, even though I cursed a lot.

"Most guys are assholes, Alida. You gotta find one of the few who isn't."

For as long as I've been dating, I've been attracted to assholes, and my brother knows it. If there is one thing I blame, it is what I have termed the *Shawn Hunter phenomenon*. You guys watched *Boy Meets World*, right? Shawn is single-handedly responsible for why I consistently date terrible, unavailable guys. In case you haven't seen the show, the lead character is a "nice" guy named Cory. An obnoxious trick birthday candle of a man, he has loved the same girl since he was six, has that *work out for him*, and never knows anything but comfort and a strong familial unit and stupid hair. Nice guys have it good, we all learned, and yet look how annoying they are! Cory was whiny and spoiled, and always making terrible jokes like some hack comedian in the Catskills. His best friend Shawn, on the other hand, provided the necessary balance to Cory.

Shawn was a blazing forest fire, always combing his hands through his floppy hair, showing a slight disrespect for school authority, and, like any bad boy, wore gold chains. He spelled his name rebelliously, his foster father had a motorcycle and an earring, and he cut all the sleeves off everything he owned. It was love at first sight for girls of the '90s everywhere, a collective girl sigh rippling through households whenever he showed up on screen with his trademark plaid and pout. Shawn was an adolescent god, our generation's Judd Nelson, the ultimate bad boy. He was the star; Cory was the square, a guy who no doubt grew up to be an avid reader of the *Wall Street Journal*. Shawn was the first boy I truly lusted for, my adolescent hormones awakened like a baby cat opening its eyes for the first time. He created an ideal I held for seven years and into syndication.

The Shawn Hunter phenomenon is how I've romantically destroyed myself over the years. Now, Shawn is replaced by every guy who smells woodsy, loves Tom Waits, and has a voice that sounds like whiskey and cigarettes. I want nothing more than to be the Angela to someone's Shawn; to be the cool girl who makes the bad boy realize that love is possible and worth it. Looking back, I wish I had just watched *The Brady Bunch* as a kid and looked for guys with resilient attitudes toward divorce, but no-go. *Boy Meets World* set me on a warpath to falling for men who would never call me, and I could not assume it was because he was hanging out with his elderly principal.

I tried to explain the Shawn Hunter phenomenon to my brother, that nice wasn't a *bad* thing, but it wasn't exciting, and goddammit, I wanted adventures! He dismissed me with a wave of his hand.

"Think of the guys you dated, Alida. They were *awful to you*. Jeez. It's like you've gotten used to it."

It was true. In my college years, I had a talent for finding guys with emotional issues, with acoustic guitars, with anger, or with girlfriends they didn't tell me about. They disappointed me one after the other, until I was so immune to terrible behavior that I expected it and sought it out. My heart was protected by a rib cage as anatomy deemed, a rib cage that participated in the occasional sex romp with the kind of men who didn't want to talk about their day with me, let alone take me home to Mom. It had become routine for me to expect the least of the men I dated.

And it didn't get better after college. In fact, when I was meeting with my brother, I had just recently been dumped by a guy named Trevor, a complete asshole I met at a bar who was excellent at making jokes. He was my first after-college romance, a relationship that was defined mostly by his indifference, his inability to give me compliments, his scrutiny of my outfits, his attractive face, and our habit of texting each other more than seeing each other in person.

Trevor's awful behavior was no surprise to any of my friends, or to me, really. As much as I crave bad boys, I also crave some sort of predictable aspect to my life. I had this destruction down pat. Keeping around a guy I met at a bar (in this case, a guy who within hours of meeting told me he had never bought anything for a girl) was commonplace behavior. It allowed me to feel the old familiar feelings—attract them with my humor and my blasé attitude and my quick insults. Get immediately excited when he mentions he's been to jail for fighting. Admire his leather jacket while making out with him. Watch him as he scoffs at human kindness, carries existential books around, and announces he doesn't believe in labels. Assume that he will immediately fall head over heels regardless. Realize that his being sarcastic toward me has transformed him into being a jackass only to me. Tell my friends I am okay, I might see him this weekend, but who knows where he goes. Listen, oddly detached, as he talks about other girls. Never want him to meet my friends. Get nervous when he raises his voice. Still text him constantly. Convince myself that the challenge is worth it, have little victories when he texts me first or asks me to hang out first or lifts his finger in the slightest way. Feel myself getting annoyed but deciding to stick it out. Put up with some more bullshit. Realize he's not a badass, he gets money from his parents. Realize his leather jacket is pleather. Decide not to text him first again, see what happens. Never see him again.

Boom! I just did that off the top of my head.

"Why exactly do you find yourself attracted to assholes?" my brother asks. The beers have turned him into a goddamn armchair psychiatrist, and I am the patient who has been committed against my will.

I take a moment to reflect. In my defense, most breakups occur because they aren't the right fit, not because the people are terrible, spirit-crushing humans. There are a million shades of wrong for a particular person, and not every shade is awful. But there are people who are *more* wrong for a person than others, and I seem to have found a surplus of men who are bold, capitalized, underlined *wrong* for me.

Memories flashed before my eyes, a bunch of men who

never asked anything of me because they never wanted to give anything in return. An old high school flame, a dropout who liked drugs more than he liked me, who was honest about seeing other girls because he knew he could be, and who made me laugh and so I put up with bad behavior. The first guy who broke my heart, a guy with gauges in his ears, who cheated and lied and hinted at it, but I still cried. A college boyfriend with whom things went awry because we stopped making fun of each other and became polite and tired. Guys who faded out of the picture because they were mean or inconsiderate or bored or cornered.

And then there's me, terribly afraid to step out of the box and date someone different. Afraid to get hurt in a different, more complex way—by somebody who I *actually* trust and care about. My biggest fear. *Nice* guy was a bad word to me because I feared that lurching-stomach feeling of losing someone I love. *Nice* meant *future*, and the future was always uncertain.

I don't explain this fear to my brother, instead telling him that yes, I realize that, in all honesty, I am not even the kind of girl who *should* be dating bad boys. I don't have a Russian-model body that is good for wearing catsuits and being in Bond movies, I don't like how loud guns are, and I spill things on myself constantly. It's just nice to think you know what you don't want and do want in somebody. It's just nice to know what to expect, even if it is bad.

"You're smart." He concludes, "One day, you'll be ready to find somebody better."

★　　★　　★

Not every girl has a bad-boy problem. Some of my friends get into relationships constantly. Others cheat all the time, or run away. Some get jealous. Some think they are too undateable to even try. Our dating pool is a circus of fuckups, misfits, and past mistakes that we keep on making. The brand of baggage you're carrying on your back is the issue. But most of all, I think we fear the same thing.

I think that thing is love. *Real* love.

Think of your first love. Think of how Bambi-like you were, prancing around all excited and in love with everything. Then think of how that happiness was beaten to death with a hatchet, spit on, shit on, leaving you cold. If you watch something you care about get destroyed, you're not going to want to go back to that place, no matter how pleasant it ever was. I can tell you right now that I fuck up because the idea of that brief happiness, followed by the agony of the Band-Aid being ripped off? That's scarier than anything. That's scarier than missing texts from somebody you wouldn't expect to send you one anyway.

In movies, there are always obstacles. There are always bad boys before the storm, some terrible schmuck who ruins the main character and makes her tired but ever closer to finding that somebody who will wake her up. There is plenty of suffering before the good happens. This is something that I have taken stock in, because I've dealt with plenty of bullshit for somebody so fresh out of the womb. I deal with the difficult

because I expect, in return, a reward down the line. I believe
in the eventual payoff, and I also believe in paying your dues.
That payoff, I reason, will be so huge. You deal with the
worst, you get the best. I want big emotions and orchestral
music and a very real commitment in the two of us. That
takes some trial and error. That takes some patience. That
takes things I was not ready to give yet—my all.

It'll never happen with any of my bad boys. Bad boys will
never want to loaf on a couch with me without the promise
of robbing a bank later. They have never understood me, even
though it seemed like they could, on account of all my tough-
looking jackets. We were always two cool ships passing in the
night, because I called my mother and thought that being
considerate to people was important. They didn't.

There would be somebody else, when I was open enough
for the situation to mosey its way on over to me. This guy
wouldn't be nice. He would be cool AND kind, and nobody
would ever call him nice because they were too busy calling
him funny. I would meet him after a long string of rude people, and he would be fresh air after a whole lot of smoke. I
would be so grateful for him to be there. I would tell him,
"Nobody's been so good to me," and I would really, really
mean it. However, like the movie heroine who doesn't know
she's going to end up with the guy right in front of her, you
have to do the audience a favor and open up your fucking
eyes to what was around you.

Life is not a movie. No happy ending is guaranteed. No
wound is closed by magic. There had been lessons I had been

refusing to learn. How if you aren't letting somebody know they're hurting you, they'll keep doing it. How if you aren't letting yourself know you're hurting yourself, you'll keep dating assholes. How, honey, you really need to stop dating assholes. That shit is not cute. Acknowledging them is half the battle.

My brother and I went out for beers a few weeks after our initial conversation. I wanted to let him know that I had taken his advice seriously and I wanted to try something with him.

"You know, I cry sometimes." I begin with a strong, embarrassing point and keep on going with the revelations. "I help old ladies cross the street. I get emotionally invested in animals. I smile and give hugs to my friends, and I don't like making people feel bad. I am a nice girl, and no matter how tough I think I am, I hate getting hurt. I am Alida," I say, "and I deserve to meet somebody who I can trust. Somebody who sees me like my brother sees me: a great girl. Worthy of a return phone call."

My brother nods slowly.

"Well," I continue, "he has to be, like, not a wimp or anything. And he has to be able to at least *watch* horror movies with me. I'm not going to date somebody who has the personality of a shoehorn because they'll buy me dinner. I'm not saying you're right and I'm going to forever date nice boring suit types. I need some substance. You know, maybe not a *challenge*, but somebody who keeps me guessing. With their jokes! Who, okay, probably didn't take revenge for his father's death. . . ."

"Uh, Alida. Why don't we see?"

My brother smiles, stretches, relishing in a point he'd been trying to make since I had braces. We go back to drinking and I call him an asshole sixteen times, a term of endearment I had given to the brother who would always protect me, who always thinks that I should get the best of everything. He couldn't always be there to give that to me, though. Even the toughest of brothers can't make their sister change the things they think they are entitled to. They can't move you away from the jerks. They can simply hold their breath and their baseball bat.

"You don't need a nice guy, Alida. You need a fuckin' *good* guy. Hell, you need a wiseass. Lots of girls need those, especially you."

He's ragging on me, so I do it right back to him. I tell him one day, he'll meet somebody who makes him constantly check his phone, makes him feel nervous when it doesn't vibrate, and makes him stick around. He tells me he won't. He and I might fall in different ways, but the idea of something real and huge—one that could potentially hurt us—was something we both were a bit scared of.

He and I will get better at this, I think. One day, we'll get beers with two more people at the table, two more people who proved us both wrong.

Drop My Keys in a Place
I Call My Own

When you live in a walk-up apartment, you learn a couple of things about yourself, and most of those things have to do with how out of shape you are. It takes me approximately fifty-two steps to get to the door of my apartment, and by the time I get up there, I'm panting. I do not want my roommates to know that I get out of breath from walking up stairs because I have been talking about "going running" forever, while completely avoiding the actual act of "starting to go running, ever." On this particular day in June, I linger outside the door, trying to control my breath. I turn off my music because you can hear that I'm listening to pop music and not something punky and cool, and then proceed to wipe my feet on my neighbor's doormat. My roommates and I have the best of intentions, but after a year of living in our apartment, nobody has remembered to pick up a welcome mat. We're always quickly and quietly shuffling our feet at the door of apartment 4E, hoping our neighbors never catch us.

I push the door open, throw my keys down, and walk across the gritty kitchen floor. "Yikes," I think, as I do a mental calculation of how long it's been since the floor was last Swiffered. My guess is at least a month. I tell myself I'll do it, but *later*, and kick off my shoes, punting them across the room because nobody is looking. Like most "first" apartments in the city, mine is dingy but comforting. There are no windows in the living room. The couch pillows smell like somebody who might have slept on them for three days, months ago. There is no "aesthetic" to my home. There are no lively vases or decorative key-lime candles. We have one picture frame: a plastic one with a picture of Fabolous in it that my friend stole at a party. We have a single wall decoration, a lizard sculpture. We constantly talk about going to IKEA without ever taking the initiative to look up how to get there.

I flop down on the couch, sip some Sprite that I had left out from the night before, and turn on the television to watch something I've probably already seen a million times. My forehead is dripping sweat and I freak out for a second when I think I see a bug out of the corner of my eye. Just my tweezers, though. I had dropped them there days ago, and don't judge the laziness implied by the second half of this sentence, but I do not pick them up because I can never find them when I put them away. The apartment smells like dumplings (Trader Joe's, $3.99), and it makes me hungry. I wonder if it's worth the effort to boil water to make pasta.

My roommate Adam enters the apartment, all plaid-shirted and red-cheeked and enthusiastic. Adam is enthusiastic and fun even when he is *not* being enthusiastic, like when he is unloading the dishwasher. His boyfriend is walking behind him; he's here almost constantly these days, and nobody minds because he always encourages popcorn making, and plus, we are adults, and adults have their boyfriends over all the time. This is just what we do now.

Adam plops his keys into the octopus candleholder (which obviously has never once held a candle) and pulls an envelope from his back pocket.

"We got our lease renewal. We need to decide ASAP if we want to live here next year."

How was your day? Hello, what do you want for dinner?

I answer those questions in my head and then I decide to address the only thing he actually asked.

"We should talk about it together," I say.

Together being Amanda, the third roommate, the other college compadre, the other piece to the puzzle of "Should we start buying toilet paper in bulk?" Amanda is in her room, her legs strewn across her bed, shorts on, scrolling down a Web site on her Mac keypad with one finger. She has moisturized, I imagine, the only one of us who can do that consistently. We tell her the news; she agrees we need to sit down and discuss soon.

I go back to the couch and sink into its mustiness. I close my eyes and think of nothing, like how much money I have or how to move a bed down fifty-two steps.

★　　★　　★

One year and four months prior to that day, I was green and
naïve and liked to do plenty of things I don't like to do
now—eat sushi, buy posters to hang up, look for apartments.
I had money in my bank account and was ready to move out
of my childhood home into my "own pad," which would
eventually lead to a "bigger place," and then "a place with the
[not yet real] boyfriend" and eventually a 401(k) and a future
where I was nostalgic for my twenties. A springboard into
real life!

I took the steps needed—I told my parents I would be
leaving, and then begged for them to help me move. I looked
for friends who would also be willing to move with me, pref-
erably ones who didn't use check-cashing stores. Through
casual and distracted Internet chatting and overly enthusiastic
drunk texts, two former roommates and I decided to take the
plunge together.

This was good, I reasoned. Living with people you had
already lived with before means you never really have to im-
prove yourself as a roommate. Nobody would ever expect me
to open the mailbox ever or remember to turn off the light
when I went to bed. In turn, I didn't expect them to do
something insane and obnoxious like date a standup comic,
and I wouldn't complain if they never cleaned the bathtub. It
was a sweet deal, a much-needed reprieve from trying to find
Craigslist roommates who didn't sound like they followed
people in parking lots or, even worse, were in a band that
would practice in the apartment.

The three of us began to chatter about "THE MOVE"

before we even started to look for apartments. We thought of THE MOVE in terms of getting boyfriends at the exact same time, or eventually commuting to work in nice outfits we didn't have, or getting home after a long night of listening to the bumping music that I'd probably consider grating a year later. Like I said, naïve.

The first time we looked for apartments, we met up beforehand and laid down our guidelines, the same way children ramble on and on about game rules they make up on the spot: Subway proximity. Closets. No muggings. Privacy. A balcony, maybe. Wood floors. Cute neighbors. A good bar nearby. Affordable. Working toilet. Laundry in the basement. Personally, I cared only about the not-getting-mugged part. I imagined that criminals would sense that I had my own place and immediately jump out of bushes and take my tiny Target purse, laughing as I yelled "Stop that man!" to no avail.

We settled on a reasonable rent range, based on no knowledge of how much it costs to do anything. We thought our electric bill would be something in the vicinity of "You know, it's not like we keep our lights on that often. Just at like, you know. Night." We were *excited* to spend money. We were excited about "up-and-coming" neighborhoods where we stuck out like sore thumbs on hands that could not defend from a potential attacker. We pretended not to care that *up-and-coming* meant *look at this one hipster coffee shop to satisfy you, you spoiled pig brat*. We were excited about the potential of any neighborhood—of finding brunch places and bartenders who would say, "Hey, how is that [insert personal thing he knows about you here]," and good bodegas.

Green. Green. Green.

We had lists of Craigslist Realtors printed out, numbers that we would call, and a Juán or Joe or Jack would put us on hold and ask us if we would consider paying just a *little* more than our agreed maximum. A little would be more like a thousand. All the Realtors looked like they were the kinds of guys who hit on women at bars by peacocking, like they read *The Game*. They would leer at us with eyes full of dollar signs and shinier ties than I would have ever trusted otherwise. Most were around our age, or wanted to be. It goes without saying that people our age don't know *shit*.

We found ourselves unsuccessful on more than one million occasions. Two weeks stretched into months and season changes and apartments that didn't "really have walls." (Yes, that's right. An apartment with no bedroom walls.) Once, we waited for close to an hour outside a head shop for a landlord to let us up the stairs, until we noticed the fire marshall had actually shut the building down. We would sit in pizza places and glare at each other, three friends who disagreed on Realtor fees and how annoying it would be to live under a subway. I put Parmesan on my slices, they put red pepper. Would it ever work?

"I need to get out *immediately*, you guys. My parents are becoming interested in finding the URL to my personal blog," I would whine.

"Are you kidding me? It takes me over an *hour* to get into

Manhattan. How can I ever have fun when I constantly have to commute a billion hours a day?" Adam lived in Brooklyn, but not in the part of Brooklyn that was filled with young folks and not extremely old and Orthodox Jewish people.

"Guys, come on. We'll settle for the first decent apartment we see."

So we lowered the bar. Shadier neighborhoods. Less amenities. Places with visible mice.

"Maybe this is what hell is," I said on more than one occasion, knowing I was being too dramatic. This was a privilege, a luxury to be able to look for apartments in one of the best cities in the world. Going through all of this bullshit was annoying but necessary, like waiting in doctors' offices or filling out forms or cleaning our closets. But knowing that certainly didn't make it *easy*. It was a constant roller coaster of hope and disappointment, leading me to become more emotional than I ever thought I could be over a living space. I cried over my bank account and Realtor fees twice. I cried over Park Slope and small bedrooms and the Q train. I cried, and I cried, and then, the heavens opened up, after six apartments on a Sunday afternoon and iced coffee and burned bagels. Heaven in the form of a walk-up in a neighborhood I had looked at on a whim, near a church with graffiti of fruit.

When you find an apartment you are meant to be living in, the heart knows. I wanted to kiss the exposed brick, the high ceilings, or the Realtor who brought his pug and looked to be about twenty-six years old. I wanted to kiss the paper that made me hand over twenty-four hundred dollars I barely had, to live in a room that had a closet on the outside and could barely fit my twin bed. Floors that were water damaged. A new dishwasher, still in it's wrapping. It somehow arrived broken, and my dad had to fix it.

After signing the seventeen-month lease and forking over the eighty million dollars necessary to move into this place, the three of us went to a Thai restaurant, feeling celebratory and tired, like we had crossed the finish line, even though we had just begun.

"Here's to our new apartment! Here's to squalor!" We ate our pad thai, and I noticed how, when you're in the middle of them, even the biggest moments don't feel like that much at all.

The day we moved I wore a sweatshirt I used to wear a lot in high school. My parents surveyed the neighborhood and one coffee shop, two friendly elderly Hispanic men, and a Pomeranian later, they decided they would lose only a minimum amount of sleep because their daughter was moving to a mildly safe neighborhood. Then we spent three hours trying to fight the unfortunate curve in the staircase—the great mattress fight became the big dresser-drawer fight, which turned into the bed-frame fight, which turned into a white T-shirt flag of concession and back pain and armpit stains. I wiped my brow and put my hands on my hips to assess the progress every ten minutes, and it made absolutely no difference at all. I had forgotten to bring important things like my DVD collection, an extensive collection that had at least three Topher Grace films. Even without the weight of *In Good Company*, my limbs hurt for three days afterward. My dad hurt his back something fierce. I am too old for my dad to be helping me move, but I was too young to admit this out loud.

That night, my roommates and I drank SoCo out of our mismatching glasses and cheered to absolutely nothing. To sleep. To unpacking. We stared at the boxes and unpacked and half unpacked things and said to ourselves, *This is the beginning of something!*

Something, of course, that would eventually turn into the everydayness, the usual, the routine of life that we wait for blips of excitement in.

By the time the second summer in our apartment rolled around, we weren't so enamored with our living conditions. The bathroom wouldn't stop smelling like mold, but by cracking the tiny window, our neighbors could see us showering, so we kept it closed and held our breath when it got too rancid. One day, the tub filled up quickly and the water wouldn't go down. I peered into the murky, foggy water and looked for any sign of the swirl and drain. Nothing. I came back twenty minutes later. There was my hair, Amanda's hair, all kinds of hair floating in the tub. I texted our super, Angel, or Super Angel, as we call him, and he told me he would come fix it. He did not, so I showered in hair and skin and volumizing shampoo. The second day, I decided to take matters into my own hands and poured a whole bottle of Drano down the drain until it went down halfway. I felt triumphant, capable, until I saw a water bug and stood on the sides of the tub, like the ground was splitting beneath me, to wash my hair.

I counted six cockroaches that summer. The first time, it climbed into my shoe and I screamed until Adam killed it. The next time, I hit it with a wine bottle until it split in half, the disembodied creature moving its legs until I covered it with a tissue.

The freezer stopped working and my Fudgsicles became liquid, so I had to pour it into a cup and drink it. It doesn't even fill the glass up a quarter of the way, and it's not refreshing, and it is so hot in our apartment that my boyfriend, my very first city boyfriend, tells me to come to his house on weeknights. He comes on weekends, and I have to give him glasses of wine and then he falls asleep.

"I hate this apartment," I would say, and then remembering the parties we hosted, the good times laughing with the roommates, the idea that this place was my *home*, I'd take it back.

Amanda, Adam, and I are sitting in a Venezuelan bar that is twenty minutes from home. We have all met up after work and our feet are tired from walking in shoes that pinch our toes or don't support our heels, because we are young and stupid and think about form over function. We are here to eat mini sandwiches and drink margaritas and talk about the apartment.

On sunny, nice days, we had talked about checking out different neighborhoods, but on nice, sunny days, the last thing we wanted to do was look for apartments. Deep in their brains, there is one thing every city dweller knows. If you actually are serious about apartment hunting, you have to do it before your lease dries up, or else you'll end up in a wall-less, closetless apartment with a roommate who has a Wii Fit and insomnia.

We think of the mice and the cockroaches and the fact that sometimes our whole place smells like mold. Balance out the positives and negatives.

"I think we should stay another year." I don't remember who said it. We all sighed.

Adam takes out the lease, and I take out a pen from my purse to sign it.

This time, we cheer to remaining the same. Another year of breaking things and no windows. A closet on the outside, in the living room. We are relieved not to have to experience change again so soon. There will be time to do that later, when the idea of moving seems exciting and affordable, not scary and impossible.

"You know," I say, a mouth full of black beans, "we should probably go to IKEA."

Thoughts on Being Dragged to a Bar by Your Friends Who Are Concerned for Your Well-Being

When you're in your twenties and you want to do something on a Saturday night, you pretty much have two options. You either go out drinking or you sit in your pajamas and stay at home. I don't have a problem with sitting at home. It's something I've completely mastered—you make yourself some fried eggs, dance alone to music, and imagine you are an elf from *The Lord of the Rings* as you shoot imaginary arrows into the air. It's basic slothing 101, elementary, my dear Watsons.

I have been known to stay in many a night. I find consecutive nights out tiring, and eating cereal while standing up so goddamn appealing. Apparently, too much of this behavior can come off as "kind of sad" to people. "Come out, Alida," my friends say. "You live in this beautiful city!" I know, I know. Lord knows I like drinking enough, it's just that sometimes drinking in public seems so *boring*. Sure, there are people out there I could meet who have interesting and provocative things to say, but sometimes I think I'd prefer to do something stupid, like buy a hermit crab and feed it stuff, rather than listen to some guy yammer on about his feelings on socialized health care. What can I say? I have low expectations for what social situations can bring.

I blame television for all of this, mostly because I like to sit at home and watch it instead of doing anything else. I trust television, because I know what to expect from it. I like that I can turn it on and there will be a show that portrays high school as a place where beautiful twenty-five-year-olds with amazing clothes have sex all the time or a festering hellhole where everybody gets harassed online. For girls to wear sparkle dresses and get into awkward situations with men. For girls with glasses to make jokes. For Asians to be underrepresented. For cops to throw away the book. For AMC to be the best.

It should come as no surprise, then, that I'd rather stay in and turn on the ole tube than go out and meet folks. I know at least forty-five people. This feels like enough for me. Not so, says society! Go out there and get drunk and have an okay time, but do it because it's expected of you and your youthful liver!

To make myself feel a little better about the decrepit, degenerate life I lead, I'm going to describe it to you imagined in the form of entertainment that I love so much. Given that I am an underemployed college graduate who has a little bit of experience in screenwriting, I thought I'd try my hand on a little script for you. A night out in the eyes of me.

What the fuck else am I supposed to be doing with my time? My hair is mousy brown and I'm four feet, eleven inches; I'm certainly not going to go out there and *model*. The funny monkey will make funny monkey jokes for you, because there are lots of girls making jokes on television and I deserve to have my chance, too.

Here we go! You might be surprised! Or disgusted! You'll probably be disgusted.

An Anatomy of a Night Out or: The Slightly Dissatisfied Generation

SCENE: A small room in Williamsburg, Brooklyn, on a Saturday night. The bed remains unmade, and on that bed sits ALIDA in pajamas, hair almost dry as she furiously scrunches it with drugstore mousse, over her computer. She is engrossed in Facebook, growling over the fact that somebody else has gotten engaged. JIM and JANE look nauseatingly happy, and it's enough to make her scratch at both her own arms and the computer. She growls like a rabid but harmless lapdog as she stares at the timeline of the last guy who rejected her, a complete asshole she'd be willing to take back if he just stopped RUNNING FROM "US."

A V<small>OICE</small>, *urgent.* Are you READY to go yet?

A<small>LIDA</small>, *annoyed.* Yes! I am almost completely ready, but you cannot come in because I am putting on underwear! Do not enter my room, because you will see me naked or at the very least, expose my egregious lie of being almost ready. (*She gets up from her computer chair, lazily putting on deodorant and deciding which one of her twenty-dollar dresses she should wear. She shoves on her "base coat," which is cleanish underwear and the least ripped of her black tights. She picks up some clothes and throws them on the floor. A Pitbull song can be heard from the living room, hoping to lure the siren ALIDA from her safety cave of wonders.*)

A<small>LIDA</small>. God DAMN it! (*Alida is stuck in one of her dresses. It is over her head and she is waving her arms like one of those wavy blow-up men that are used outside electronic stores and car dealerships. She has accidentally gotten deodorant marks all over the front, and finally, she rips it off and is now sweating profusely. Dress #2 has something tacky like leopard print on it, a trend that is popular with both cougars and the youth they try to steal life energy from. She stares at herself sideways in the mirror and realizes she has taco gut, not surprising, considering she has just eaten a lot of tacos.*)

ALIDA, *to herself*. If I stand precisely
like this with my hands on my hips the
ENTIRE night and never sit down and never
breathe, I look pretty good in this dress.
Pret-ty, Pret-ty good. (*She feels sad she
doesn't know Larry David.*)

VOICE. Come on! We're doing shots! (*While
the sweet nectar of alcohol does tempt her,
ALIDA must put her makeup on first. She
loads up on her drugstore eye shadow,
vigorously applying it until she gets her
eyes as smoky and cheap as a dive bar in
Philadelphia. She looks like a fourteen-
year-old experimenting with makeup, which
she decides might work for some people. A
leather jacket will make this whole thing
cool, she decides. She emerges from the
bedroom and does a spin.*)

FRIEND 1. You look great! (*Friend looks
way better.*)

FRIEND 2. You're going to be cold. (*Friend
looks way colder.*)

Alida. Pass me the whiskey. I am way too
sober to be leaving this house right now. I
am worried about real things, like how I
will never be in the Olympics and how the
hole in my heart is expanding relentlessly.
I would like to be bombed to the point
where I might believe I could have fun
tonight.

FRIEND 1. It'll be a good time. I just

need to forget about work. I need to forget about the five days a week I slave away to pay my exorbitant rent in this town full of plaid-wearing assholes who don't notice me. I am miserable because I am living an exciting, interesting, urban life.

FRIEND 2. Miserable looks GREAT on you. LADDDDIESS!

ALIDA. There once was a time I used my brain for things like reading and expanding my brain. I just thought I'd throw that out there before I put on the television and get absorbed in something like *P.S. I Love You.*

FRIEND 2. We should take a shot to the Internet! It keeps our brains so *fresh*!

FRIEND 1. How youthful of you to say! Thank god for your youth! We should take a shot to our youth! It allows us to be snappy and fresh and do things like wear high-waisted pants and make pop-culture references.

ALIDA. Despair at leaving the house peppered with a *Daria* or *Dr. Who* reference. (*Audience goes wild, they love the joke.*)

FRIEND 1, *a hopelessly optimistic idiotic tone.* Maybe you'll meet somebody tonight!

FRIEND 2. Yeah. I bet there's probably some guy out there who smirks a lot and enjoys the same movies as you or something. Something NICE could happen!! (*Hysterical laughter, uncontrollable with the slightest* tinge of sadness. A cruel inside joke that everybody is in on. *The audience gives a knowing sigh of "Oh THIS won't go well," kind of like whenever Tim Allen picks up a tool in* Home Improvement. *He NEVER improved his home! EVER!*)

ALL. To nice things! (*All the ladies take a shot to "nice things," which none of them believe, and they choke on the alcohol and sputter because it's bottom-shelf poison.*)

ALIDA. Should we cheers to something like SEX? We're modern women! Don't we have a lot of SEX or something? (*The audience LOSES THEIR MIND IN LAUGHTER.*)

FRIEND 1. Oh, Alida. I forgot to tell you. (*She looks nervous.*) We're leaving the BK womb tonight. We're going into Manhattan.

ALIDA. NOOOOOOOOOOOOOOOOOOOOOO! (*The camera pans out to her being rained on, staring at the mad gods in the sky before she calms down.*) It's fine, really. Different day, same shit. I only get indignant about Manhattan because it feels good to have a staunch opinion on something. Huzzah! (*All three look down sadly at their shoes and drink chasers and repeat this at least four times before they put on their coats and go out into the terrifying night. They spend twenty minutes trying to find a cab before resigning to the subway.*)

ANNOUNCER. The L train to Manhattan will

depart in the next 834 minutes. (*The girls
sit on the train while a crackhead sits on
a baby, a couple simulates oral sex, and a
group of drunk teenagers throw Mountain Dew
at old women.*)

SCENE: A bar in Manhattan, but it's not one
of those trendy cool bars you've seen on
television. It's a sticky, crowded bar
filled with more people than a Boston
University stadium, which is ironic because
most of these men went to Boston
University. Men with hair gel are making
gorilla noises. The bouncer wants so badly
to be put out of his misery, he's stopped
stamping people's hands and just gives them
copies of his suicide note. The bar is a
hot plate of bodies looking to do it or to
smoke cigarettes in public and spend too
much money on beer. It's gross and smells
like Heineken-y piss. (*The three ladies
enter.*)

    FRIEND 1. Glad I wore this tight dress
that everybody can see in this horrifyingly
red light. The red light makes me feel like
a hooker.

    FRIEND 2. With a heart of gold? (*All
silently praise Julia Roberts as they push
past a sea of girls in crop tops and a*

bunch of guys constantly high-fiving each
other over poon jokes.)

ALIDA, *to the bartender who looks
miserable and endlessly cool.* I'll take a
DRINK, please. I'll pay with my credit card
because I have no money. (*Listens to
bartender.*) Yes. I have almost NO money.
Yes, I'm aware of the irony of this.
(*Listens.*) Mhmmm. I AM a worthless,
floating entity. Thanks for the beverage.
(*Takes a victory sip like an asshole.*)

FRIEND 1. If you'd like, we could get into
an entirely drunken political discussion
where I could pepper in anecdotes about my
college classes. That might be fun and
stimulating because I can hear almost
nothing in this place except my own
thoughts.

ALIDA. I get that. My education makes me
entirely qualified to discuss a bunch of
important things—take my three papers
devoted to the racial other in *Jane Eyre*.

FRIEND 2. Oh, that's weird. I wrote almost
fourteen papers on the feminist perspective
in *Jane Eyre*.

FRIEND 1. I love discussing feminism. Or
the economic upswing. Or Taylor Swift. I
could go on.

ALIDA. I'm so worried my mind is going
away and melting and disappearing.

ALL. That's because it IS! (*Clink their drinks together in unison. The sounds of Dubstep makes them all have an instant panic attack.*)

FRIEND 1. How often do you think about things like VACATION homes?

ALIDA. We are the future 1 percent! (*Audience groans.*) No. NO. I'm an artist. I'll start a zine or something. Let's sit here on this bench and discuss future art projects.

ENTIRE BAR. Three cheers for blogs! (*At this point, a beautiful man approaches them. His smile holds secrets and a million sunsets. He is wearing great shoes. Everybody's heart stops. He walks past them and goes to his girlfriend. Behind him appears a great orangutan of a man—sweaty and sleazy and dripping. He goes straight to Friend 1, and then his even grosser friend, a great SLUG of a man, approaches ALIDA.*)

SLUG. I WAS going to say something about your butt, maybe.

ALIDA. Interesting. Tell me MORE, please.

SLUG. Oh. You're one of those FUNNY girls. You make jokes?

ALIDA. Yes. Isn't it amazing? Women can joke nowadays!

SLUG. Do your glasses mean I can't bone you? Will you take them off during "doin' it?"

ALIDA. Oddly, sometimes I keep them on.
I'm going to look really bored now in the
hopes that somebody will throw salt on you
and you explode.

SLUG. You got quite the wall up there,
kid. Can't some guy at a bar just come up
to you and try to get you to make out? (*He
begins to secrete slime. Will any girl ever
write a touching acoustic guitar song about
him? The world might never know.*)

ALIDA. I have to pee. Please don't ask for
my number. (*Alida waits on the line for
twenty minutes while her bladder stages a
full-on rebellion against the rest of her
body. She begins to pull out her phone to
text because she's a self-harming moron.*)

TEXT 1, *emotionally unavailable guy she
flirts with.* So b00red at bar. Please like
me. PLEASE?

TEXT 2, *crush she hopes to one day make
out with in the corner of some dark Spanish
restaurant.* I H8 people. Doesn't the fact
that I hate people make me so interesting
and attractive in my cynicism? Please want
to kiss me.

TEXT 3, *friend who will definitely text
her back so she can at least feel the
comfortable buzz of the phone in her
pocket.* I 19ve you! Please let me feel
loved. (*Alida squats in the river of toilet
paper and STDs. The mirror reveals a face*

she does not recognize, and she realizes she is due for another eight drinks. Hopefully, this time, the despair won't immediately kick in. Hopefully a television character will be real in this bar and love her.)

GIRL CRYING AT BAR. I'm sad because of a guy!

ALIDA, *shakes her.* You're sad because this is your life!!

ADORABLE GAY MAN. Yay!

ALIDA. I don't want to marginalize you or anything, but FINALLY, somebody I can talk to!

GIRL WHO GETS MAD BECAUSE ALIDA BUMPED INTO HER. EGGGHHH.

BARTENDER. Fifteen-dollar minimum!

ALIDA. Thirty more drinks, please! (*She generously buys a Yuengling for a friend in need. A brief sadness fills her as she walks back to her friends. Is this what makes people happy now? She notices all of the people laughing and losing their debit cards. It's a sea of people who LOOK happy, at least. Let's not get Plath on this shit, she thinks. Maybe she should smile or something.*)

FRIEND 2. You wanna go outside and smoke?

ALIDA. Do you want to talk about EMOTIONS or something? It seems like you might want to talk about feelings. (*Friend 2 vigorously*

nods as Friend 1 is absorbed in a
conversation with a male who seems not like
an ax murderer, because some ladies have
all the luck.)

FRIEND 2. I miss him/it/something! I have
these big emotions and they are making my
eyes fill up with tears. (*The audience does
not know where to go with this stunning
show of realness. This was supposed to be a
FUN NIGHT!*)

ALIDA. A little bit of alcohol makes me
feel good and happy. A lot makes me FEEL
THINGS. You wanna cry over something now?

FRIEND 2. It's like real talk! I'll reveal
this big secret, and then I'll cry. It'll
be great.

ALIDA. I will reveal that I have a human
heart. Let's do this. (*The two hug it out,
kind of like* Entourage, *but with more words
and less grunting.*)

FRIEND 2. Will we ever be satisfied?

ALIDA. Spoiler alert: No. But it will get
better. And it's also supposed to NOT GET
ANY BETTER THAN THIS. (*Gestures to the big
world of bars.*)

FRIEND 2. That's sad.

ALIDA. I know. I know. (*And so the night
goes, with drinks and texts and stares at
various men who will never talk to her. The
lone memory of some guy Alida wishes were
there surfaces, and at least one more*

*discussion about feelings occurs before she
heads to the subway. At home, barely
removes her makeup, has a sip or two of the
leftover mixed drink, and goes to bed. She
wakes up at 2:30 P.M. the next day to a
text.*)

ALIDA. Yeah. Sure. I'll go out tonight, I
guess. (*She shuts her phone and gets up to
take a shower. This will be the only
episode of the entire series, save for two
or three episodes where she meets somebody
who eats her heart/gets a head cold/stays
in to watch four seasons of* Curb Your
Enthusiasm.)

END SCENE.

The day will sneak up on me when I will miss this, when I have settled into an older, more mature life where I have grown in a real, tangible way. When I have joined a book club, or I am dating somebody in a way that involves real trust and real teamwork, when I have work responsibilities I am excited to tackle. When I own a pair of slacks, and whoa, *now* I'm just exaggerating. There will never be slacks. But I *will* find that other things will take precedence over Saturday nights out. They will become less frequent, and when they happen they will be in wine bars or places where people speak in normal voices. One night, wiser and older and ready to spend some of my hard-earned, well-managed cash, I'll pass a bar with a cover and look inside and see the young crowd it drew. I'll pause. I'll smile. I'll look at my companion and in one nostalgic breath, I'll speak. "Man, being younger sucked. Those nights were the worst. Sure, sometimes it was fun to go *Girls Gone Wild* with a couple of plastic shot glasses, but really, how much money could I have saved if I just stayed home? Learned about the stock market? These kids will drink themselves to smithereens. Shit, I need a cab out of this neighborhood and a '96 Pinot. I feel an episode coming on, and my psychiatrist is off in Florida." And then, if just for a moment, I'll remember the Alida of my youth, standing in the corner. Marginally miserable, if not just tired. Then I'll think to myself, *Damn. I was one smart son of a bitch back in the day.* And that will be good enough.

The Grilled Cheese That Changed My Life

I t's a Friday night, just late enough to be almost too late to leave the house, and I am running back and forth between my closet and the TV during the commercial breaks of the *Sex and the City* movie. I want to make sure I don't miss the part where Carrie gets dumped minutes before her wedding. It's my favorite part. She beats him with flowers while wearing a bird on her head and it's some Lynchian-film-student-wore-some-stilettos kinda shit. I have a handful of my new best friend—chips that are baked, not fried, and which smell like feet—and I'm sipping gin through a straw.

"Girls' night OUT," I chirp to no one. I am staring sideways into the full-length mirror after doing a quick jump-thigh shimmy-jump into a cheap black dress, checking to see if you can see the Spanx line. A pound of hairspray and fifteen layers of one-dollar wet *n* wild lipstick later, and I am ready to go. I am a shrine to Victoria's Secret fragrances. I am suck-your-stomach-in Barbie. I am tottering on high heels and hoping that nobody notices my love handles. I notice them, and I keep making dry CBS-approved jokes to the mirror about how they should call them hate handles. I am hoping nobody notices my muffin top. I notice it, and like an amateur female standup comic somewhere in Reno, I could go on for five to seven minutes about it.

I flip the channel to *Mean Girls* while I finish my drink.

"I want to lose three pounds," Regina George says.

How funny, I think, as I walk outside of my apartment, trying not to catch glimpses of myself in car mirrors. So do I.

Girls have trouble simply *hanging out*. There's always a reason for getting together, a declarative statement that ends with somebody saying, "We better just meet Friday for drinks . . . to DISCUSS." We don't just "meet for drinks" because it's Tuesday. There's always some terrifying underlying tone for the meet-up—perhaps your friend is passive-aggressively going to confront you for spending too much time with your boyfriend. Maybe you need to talk for six hours about your friends who aren't there, or what kind of haircut you should get. Perhaps your friend needs to talk for three sangria carafes about how Blake, a guy who looks like he barrel-rolled straight out of his fraternity into her arms, didn't call her this weekend (just say it: He hates her).

In this case, my friend Danielle and I decided to have one of those nights because we were sick and tired of spending hours on the Internet talking about how happy we were being single. It's all we did, like old people love talking about how they used to be young. We were raving about it *so* much that we didn't notice we had poured chocolate and hot sauce all over our pajamas and it had set in and we had become cemented to the floor. Like plants, we needed to be brought out into sunlight and watered and taken care of. We needed to leave the house to do something crazier than trying to pop a cheek pimple, and girls' night was an excellent excuse.

"We'll meet GUYS," I said. Men who wear button-down shirts and work at nonprofits or sing in bands and lean on counters and never call and make you hate yourself and possibly the human race in general!

"GUYS!" she said, as we drooled all over our computer keys, trying to remember what human touch feels like.

The moment you proclaim a girls' night out, the winds change. A glitter double rainbow, dusted with lip gloss and wedge platforms and Nicki Minaj songs, floats across the sky, and the prophecy has spoken. It doesn't matter how much dignity you have or how single you are or aren't. You're about to go on the hunt. My laugh gets higher, my nails pinker, my brain considerably less academic. Goals have been set: Make an attractive person smile while you giggle. Justify your dress and the effort you took in putting it on. End the night sending odd texts to a number you didn't have a few hours ago, making promises you won't keep, licking late-night nacho dust off your fingers. It's not your proudest night, but it's certainly *A NIGHT*.

But this one . . . it wasn't starting off on the right foot. A bad mood was settling in, the same kind of bad mood I get in whenever I am at a party and people decide to talk about sports. The pregame drinks I had didn't make me buzzed, they just made me feel irritated and groggy, my hair looked like a fuzzy mess of hay, and I was already regretting my choice to wear heels. I watched as couples around me slowly ambled by, kissing, and I wanted to beat them with broken bottles. The shrill cries of teenagers echoed in my head like they were dog whistles that brought no adorable puppies. So help me children, I thought, if one of you accidentally bumps into me, *I will end up in jail.*

Danielle met me on a street corner and we stood in the cold like idiots, debating where to go. The bars in my neighborhood fit into one of these four categories: the places you used to go when you wanted to drink underage, the seedy bars you think only exist in *Road House* ("I used to fuck guys like you in prison!"), the places that people who don't like club music go to and dry hump each other to indie music, and the Commodore (the best one, try the chicken). We ended up at the kind of underaged joint where the Absolut cocktails were inexplicably twelve dollars and a terrible band was inside playing songs about their bitchy ex-girlfriends. I started sucking down vodka like I had just walked through the desert, or spent the day at a Christian bible camp, or something else terrible, and then started on my mission— look for guys to awkwardly avoid eye contact with. Prospects weren't limited, but most were terrible. There were a few attractive guys, aloof guys who wanted you to approach them, guys with girlfriends who wore peach dresses and those preppy necklaces that looked like anal beads, guys who looked like they would make the first move but would smell very bad. I waited for somebody—ANYBODY—to talk to me. With every guy who passed me for another girl, I tried to analyze what was wrong with me. It was me, right? It was my hair. It was my glasses. It was the dress. Yeah, it was definitely because I looked chubby in this dress—my go-to reasoning for when I was feeling rejected. I needed to lose those three pounds, or five, or at least wear something that didn't hug my body so much.

After a while of yelling over the shitty music and surveying the uninterested men, Danielle and I left the bar in a huff, barely buzzed and in the kind of mood that you get in when you don't get hit on and realize it's one of those nights where you actually care about that. We went to bar after bar, sadly checking our phones in the hopes that somebody but our moms had texted us, trying specialty cocktails that tasted like piss, waiting for Godot. This night was a bust, we assumed, as we parked it at some faux Francophile establishment, surveying the crowd of Audrey Tautous with tattoos and guys who looked like you could convince them to buy a beret. My stomach began to grumble. Ah, yes, I was also in a bad mood because I was hungry, which is pretty much the only excuse both a baby and an adult can make. Danielle called over the bartender to ask for their late-night menu, and I let her know that I was trying to be good, didn't want to eat something too crazy.

The bartender was the typical booze slinger you meet in Brooklyn. Coked-out, potbelly, full of energy and animal-related skin art. He was writing a *book*, he told me. A children's book about deforestation (but I don't think it was *FernGully*). He told us to try the grilled cheese sandwich, which had approximately thirty-six kinds of cheese and bread made entirely of butter. Plus, it came with a side salad. We waffled for a minute, scanning over the other bar food choices for something that had the words *vegetable panini* in it. Soon, I realized that the grilled cheese was the best option we were going to get here. For a place that was supposed to be sophisticated, they sure did like to tout their "amazin' wings."

"I guess," I said. "Bring it out. We'll *share* it."

Girls love sharing their food. It makes us feel better about ourselves and more apt to order things that have a lot of cholesterol in them, even if we don't totally understand what cholesterol is. In my head, I told myself I wouldn't even eat all of my half. Too many calories. Think of those three pounds, Alida. I scanned the bar, looking at all of the girls who seemed impossibly thinner than I was, impossibly cooler than I was, impossibly attractive, and I started to feel even worse than I did before.

Danielle and I waited for what seemed like an eternity, before I saw a tiny Latino man waving a plate above his head, trying to get the young crowd to move the hell away from him and let him do his job. The plate bobbed through the crowd, and people started parting for it like it was Moses or Jesus making a journey through the bar. And then, there it was: the sandwich of dreams. It looked beautiful. People stopped and stared. You know the look people give people when they see a chick come down the stairs in her prom dress? This sandwich elicited the same sort of shock and awe. Williamsburg was hungry for my sandwich, and oh, it was mine!

Now, I've had some sandwiches that have changed my life: any bagel sandwich after a hangover, two-dollar *banh mi*s, and the egg and eggplant at the Clover food truck in Boston come to mind. This one, however, was a game changer. It came apart in lacy white angel strings when you pulled it, and it was crispy and grooved where it had been pressed down with butter. There were garlic pieces baked directly in with the cheese. Simply put, it looked magnificent. Danielle and I dug in, each grabbing a half. The moment we took a bite the smiling wouldn't stop, kind of like the Jack Nicholson version of the Joker. Cheese and oil and slop were dripping down our chins, but there was no time for napkins. All we kept saying was "Oh my god. This is so good. This is *so good.*" The flavors danced on my tongue and happy endorphins were surging through me. This sandwich was delicious—the holy grail of grilled cheeses. I gobbled down my half, not even touching the side salad, which I had ordered, of course, with dressing on the side. I was savoring every last drip of grease and cheese, tempted to lick the plate, and I could tell Danielle felt the same. This wasn't just a sandwich—this was a religious experience. We were purely happy in that moment, not because we were getting hit on, not because we were feeling drunk and sexy, but because of a delicious, gooey, cheesy sandwich.

A lightbulb went off in my head: *Eating food—good food, like this sandwich—is fucking worth it.*

There was a time in my life when I would've eaten every bite of that sandwich with regret, and by *time,* I mean most days of my life since adolescence. Food has always been a struggle for me—it is delicious, but it also makes my belly pooch out when I sit down, and to me, that was worse than getting diabetes or legitimate health concerns that make people cautious about their weight. Just like getting upset over idiotic nights out where you're grumpy because nobody asked for your number, worrying about gaining weight was one of those stupid, small things that feels very significant when your self-esteem is shit. And I did it all the time.

It all started—of course—in the black hole otherwise known as middle school. I was a chubby kid back then, for the same reason people railed on Snooki in season one of *Jersey Shore*—I'm short, and so my fat had nowhere to go. People made fun of me, because middle schoolers are jerks. I was weird, I was fat, I was ugly, according to what seemed like everyone. Every day was a battle to go by unnoticed. I even ate lunch in the bathroom once—yes, that actually happens to people who are bullied in real life, not just in teen dramas. Now a lot of kids are chubby in middle school, and a lot of people get made fun of in middle school. I get that. I think it's how people react to those years that sets them on a path. Do you let it affect you? Do you internalize it? For me, being made fun of introduced an even darker enemy than the kids who insulted me—and that enemy was myself. My body was the biggest villain in my life. The Bowser to my Mario. I didn't want to be known as "the fat girl," because in this world, being fat is the worst insult you could throw at a person. So I started pinching and prodding at my body in the mirror, weighing myself constantly, revolting against food—and then, poof, I started to become skinny.

By junior year of high school, all of my baby fat was gone, and I could fit into American Eagle Outfitters, size 00. Double ZERO. This really shouldn't be a thing, because we ALL have a waist size. Sometimes it's small, but it's never nonexistent. But that's what I wanted to do—to have a waist so tiny that it was almost negligible, and mostly because boys started thinking I was "pretty" and girls told me I looked really great in popped-collar polos, which is definitely a lie. I walked around with my new physique, basking in my life of having a Coach clutch, a slammin' bod to wear mall clothes on, and a boyfriend who later dumped me because he couldn't handle the stress of a traffic ticket, when the unthinkable happened.

I gained five pounds.

Holy shit, right? Five pounds! Let's all hold hands and have a candlelight vigil and throw metaphorical one-hundred-calorie snacks into the ocean and sob into each other's arms and watch eighteen-year-old me have a bit of a breakdown. Gaining these five pounds propelled me to try all sorts of EXTREME BEHAVIORS, apparently because I was a suburban half-white girl, and I needed to have some sort of eating problem or else the CW wouldn't make a show about my life.

I didn't do the grapefruit thing, or the chicken broth thing, or any other really exaggerated "insane diet thing," because my parents would notice and probably would force-feed me pork chops. But I figured out what other things I could get away with, little tricks that could get me to lose those five pounds plus a few more. Making sure I never exceeded eight hundred calories a day. Running until I needed to get physical therapy for my knee. Eating rice cakes and yogurt until I became gaunt in the face. Nobody called me out on these behaviors, because dieting is normal for teenage girls. Ordering a burger is almost more disconcerting than eating low-fat frozen meals or fiber cereal.

Even at my skinniest, I still had my hips and thighs, which drove me crazy. I would scold them in the nighttime, like they were intruders in my body Cave of Wonders. *We want our baaaagelllls,* they used to moan in the nighttime. *You're not a model, give us our creammm cheeeseee.* "Not yet!" I'd say. According to this thinspo blog I'm reading, if I eat only tubes of air and frozen grapes for another thirty-six years, I will have the photoshopped body of Adriana Lima on the cover of a woman's magazine: THINGS PHOTOSHOP CAN DO! I refused to believe that my "body type" was the reason I had hips, it was simply my inability to eat only Lean Cuisine and Splenda all day, every day. Look at all the models on the DESIGNER CLOTHES FEED ME billboards. They can do it! And look how sexual they look! *That can be me, too!*

Okay, so there's a huge difference between the high school rice cake eater (me) and the girl eating orgasmic grilled cheese (me). For one thing, I'm not nearly as apt to freak out over things as much as I did in high school, when I would have murdered somebody for turning off my television. And I also went to college and became a feminist and all that jazz, which, to me, makes the whole situation worse. I was all about women owning their body! I learned to embrace other people's fat, telling people that they should love their body, trashing magazines that pushed abs and carb cutting and millions of other stick-thin end goals. All girl bodies were great, I told myself over and over again. Except of course, mine. Mine was pretty gross.

So that's why sitting there with Danielle, eating a grilled cheese in my twenties was pretty significant. After years of believing that enjoying food made you aligned with the Dark Lord and the devil, I finally realized, that's *kind of stupid because food can be delicious*. I didn't have an "oh my god, I should stop fighting my body" moment that was so dramatic I cried. I didn't riot grrrl my way into a woman's magazine office and burn it down. I didn't grab my tummy and point at all my fat and enjoy how it kind of sticks out over my jeans. I just remembered how much I like to eat, so I ate. And I smiled. As simple as that. But that's pretty cool for a girl who used to add up all her breakfast and lunch calories on her Casio so she could see if she could eat more than a measured cup of veggie soup for dinner.

Here's the thing: I like to fucking eat. I gain immense pleasure from shoving noodles into my mouth or eating gooey slices of pizza on a Tuesday evening. Sitting there with Danielle, I realized that after years of fighting my weight, there was nothing as happy and lovely as simply enjoying food. I love the way eating *feels*, not just how *thin* feels, okay, Kate Moss?! There are some things in life that give me happiness, happiness in a way that only a scoop of ice cream can. And if that means my ribs don't stab everybody like an insane homeless person, so be it. I will gladly put up with a little bit of tummy and a little bit of thigh as long as I continue to get my precious, life-giving food. Because you NEED food to survive, but you don't NEED to be stick-fucking-thin to survive. And I'm tired, very, VERY tired, of people telling me that the women on the cover of *SEX: BE SEX* magazines are the standard of beauty. There's nothing sexier than a woman eating a sandwich, and that is my opinion, but I also suspect it is a fact. Whatever your body looks like while enjoying that sandwich? That's what your body looks like. It's the cards you've been given, lady. Thick or thin. Be as fat as you want, be as skinny as you want, but don't hurt yourself over it. Sure, you can run around and do some cardio and eat some salads if you feel crappy and unhealthy, but mostly I'd just like you to be happy and order the mashed potatoes. Go ahead. Go to a restaurant and every once in a while order the goddamn mashed potatoes. It won't kill you.

It's not a white-girl problem to want to lose weight and be a super-skinny piece of toast. It's a real problem that affects real girls who make themselves sick over lingerie models who somehow dictate how normal human beings are supposed to look. Fuck them, I say. Fuck anybody who calls anybody fat; fuck anybody who tells me that eating a good meal isn't sexy and awesome, and to any girl who thinks dieting to the point of starvation is worth having pelvic bones that stick out—it's time to grow up.

So yes, I have a tummy. I don't always love it. Sometimes I really hate it. But I am going to acknowledge it, and I'm going to deal with it. I'm going to admire it some days and I'm going to yell at it in others, but it's not going to fuck up my day.

It's not that this realization changed my life in an instant. I didn't automatically *love* my body, and I may never fully love it. And I promise you I will one day try to lose weight—maybe five pounds to fit into my wedding dress, maybe thirty pounds after I have my first kid, maybe three pounds after I find myself eating too unhealthily for a while. But I now understood that I was pretty stupid to try to hate my body, to avoid looking in mirrors. If you don't fight your body and you simply enjoy your food, you're going to be a lot better off—and I realized, finally, that that was possible for me.

And there, eating my grilled cheese sandwich with Danielle, I was much more content than if I were flirting with a dude in a synth band. We toasted to a failed girls' night and went home tired, our tummies full. The feeling of contentedness didn't last forever—these things don't change overnight. But at the moment, it was a peaceful happiness I had wanted to feel since I was twelve. No pinching. No pulling. Just happy. This feeling was better than scoring some dude's number in the back of a bar. This kind of happiness was way more filling than that.

I walk by that bar all the time now, by the way. I've never gone back in. The grilled cheese wasn't actually that good, in retrospect.

But hell, I sure enjoyed eating it.

Adventures in Retail

have been waiting for the subway for so long that I am mentally detached from the situation. I'm there, but I'm not present. I am only my body—my back facing the tunnel where the two dotted headlights will appear, the horn will honk, people will move back from the yellow line. Logically, I know that my commute is four minutes away from another transfer, but I feel as far away from my apartment as the two dogs and cat in *Homeward Bound*. I'm standing by a movie poster featuring Meryl Streep that somebody has ripped the eyes off of. Meryl can't see it, but my body is breaking its own personal record for how bedraggled it can look. My skin is covered in a thin sheen of dust, of people's complaints, of Windex, of credit card transactions, of "how can I help you"s and thirty-minute clocked-out breaks. Underneath that is a heart, one that's on guard for whole afternoons at a time, trying very hard not to lose faith in people's intelligence.

I am one of the few, the thankless, the retail workers. The one you buy your shit from, the one who has the patience of a saint, the one who sees firsthand just how little common sense the general public has. You might not see us, but boy, do we see you.

When the train finally pulls up, I grab a seat, avoiding the fleshy arms of the woman next to me. I smile at her, though I am annoyed at the intrusion of my personal space. Two men signal at me, and I think maybe I look pretty or nice or something. It is when I flit my hand to my neck do I notice that I am still wearing my name tag. I take it off, and like it has possessed me, immediately stop smiling at strangers.

I lean my head back against the edge of the seat, craving the moment I can take off my shoes and wondering how, how, I have done this for as long as I have.

The longest relationship I've ever had started at age sixteen, and it was at a coffee shop. You know the one: seven-dollar "do-it-yourself-but-somebody-else-actually-does-it" lattes and the mermaid and *come on*, it's on every corner! I won't name it because they can buy everybody I love and grind them up into 100 percent coffee smoothies. Working at this lil' company for *six years* has been the one thing I have done with the most consistency in my tiny life. Excusing my decade-long stint with playing classical piano, there has been no hobby, no boyfriend, no activity that has lasted as long as this one. You'd think that after working in the service industry for so long, it's something I would get used to—after all, besides sleeping and eating, working is certainly the thing you do the most in life.

When I started working retail in high school, I loved it. I felt important getting my own paycheck—one that I didn't need to spend on anything but movies out with girlfriends and boots I would immediately wear the heel off of. I went to school and did my homework and then I put on my uniform, pressed by my mother and brought to you by Gap work-appropriate pants, and texted all my friends "Oh, I can't go out . . . gotta work." It made me feel responsible, independent, cool. I got to yell to my parents "I go to school AND work!" My body was resilient, like all sixteen-year-old hormonal demons are, and staying on my feet for hours at a time didn't bother me at all. I flirted with all my coworkers, got them to buy me beer, drank after work in the parking lot, kissed them at parties. It felt carefree, the kind of thing that didn't have consequences—just cash and the small responsibility of showing up on time somewhere.

In college, the novelty wore off quickly. Having a full-time job while trying to figure out the pieces of your future adult life was tiring but necessary. Working at 5 A.M. and going to class just so I could live in an apartment outside of a dorm, just so I could stay afloat and go out with friends, just so I could prove to myself that I could do everything, was a badge of honor for me. The strong studied *and* got those Benjamins. The weak used "studying" as a shield for their parents' monthly bank installments. I started drinking more shots of espresso than I did rum. Sometimes I called out of work to write papers. Sometimes I skipped classes just to get some needed rest. I constantly was walking a tightrope of failing or of getting fired.

On the bad days, I would dream of giving my two weeks, but I never got around to it. Instead, I ran to the subway at 4:30 A.M. every day, propelled forward by the fear of being attacked by homeless men. I went to class wearing black button-downs. People thought I was dressed very well for a Goth, like I hated my parents but not the machine. I once had chocolate sauce on my shoes and my lit professor asked me if it was blood. I plugged on because I had grown addicted to the outside-schooling bubble. The real world was fascinating—I hated it, but I wanted to see how one survived out there. I also assumed I would get out of it after I graduated.

I've made it all sound terrible, but it wasn't. My boss was a wonderful man who was apt to cut me breaks when I showed up hungover, or who started vigorously dancing to "Take on Me" when it was slow. My best coworkers were cynical, hard-working, ball-busting godsends. I got so much free coffee I can now drink twelve shots of espresso and not even shake, so when I moved to New York I felt *pretty legit*. And, of course, I made some decent money.

The first time I went to a shift with my graduation ceremony behind me, the smiles of my coworkers were also accompanied by warnings to "go get a job, don't stay here forever." Climbing up one of the shelves to get a roll of paper towels, I was approached by a coworker. He looked me straight in the eye and said, "Kid, you really got to get yourself out of here."

This isn't the "duh" advice you might think it is. If you work retail or service, you know how easy it is to get stuck

there forever, no matter how many times you promise yourself that you will not do that. You are aware of the cycle—if
you do not hate your job, you are probably just annoyed at it,
and this is the first step to spending another five years there.
The annoyance becomes numbness, the numbness eventually
morphs into "This isn't too bad," and before you know it,
you're getting your five-year anniversary salary bump. The
feeling of "This isn't too bad, I could keep doing this" is also
owed to the terrible condition of the job market and how our
degrees can feel like they mean so little. A lot of retail jobs
offer at least some form of benefits package, and if you show
up and shut up, you get a relative feeling of security. At this
point in my life, coffee paid my bills. Coffee allowed me to
live in a nice apartment, go out on the weekends and week-
days, and go out to eat every once in a while. I was able to
save money for future loans.

But eventually, the future called to me. I hung up my apron
after more than half a decade of coffee. Moved home. Moved
to New York. Retail a distant memory, the promise of a career
laying out before me like a yellow brick road made of urgent
e-mails and morning meetings. On to other things, or so I
thought.

Fast-forward to me, a year and a half later. After scrimping and
saving on various freelance jobs, of the months of dating my
rent check a week later than when I sent it in, it became clear
that I needed more money. Taxes loomed. I needed new glasses.

I knew an easy solution, a solution that pained me and took knife swipes at my pride. Finding a full-time job was ideal, but I was gaining momentum writing and needed money more than I needed to apply to publishing jobs for months.

Not coffee, I said to myself, trying to push back the inevitable. I grew fearful of my bank account. Getting money from the ATM felt like playing Russian roulette. Freelance paychecks came weeks late. I knew how easy it would be for me to get hired at another espresso joint, how easy it would be for me to get into the routine of wearing my hair in a ponytail again.

Then, a very dull silver lining in a cloud appeared: a sign in a hip, trendy, consignment clothing store that said three bittersweet, impossible words to find. *No experience necessary.* This was my shot. I applied, cheerfully talking about my love for '90s clothing, hinting that I had no problem if they contacted my old bosses. I sent my résumé in and realized how "perfect" of a candidate I was, how qualified I was for retail.

Going in for my interview, I realized this was the first time I *needed* a job. Really, really needed it in the way that if I didn't make money soon I would have *literally no more money*. I found myself talking about my love for customer service with the kind of fervor that had never existed in the Alida of Retail Years Past. I almost convinced myself that I had forgotten how much I had loved working in retail. I ignored that this was probably creeping desperation and put all my efforts into getting this job. When you realize other people want what you are going after, you fight harder for it. And these three interviews for a barely-over-minimum-wage job told me people wanted to *work*. I was one of them. It took me two more visits with the boss, a thorough background check, a call to my references (unheard of!), and a whole lot of me actually wanting to snag the position to land it. I was relieved, celebratory. It didn't matter if this wasn't what I wanted to do in the long term, I thought, as I watched the big picture scooch over, just a bit, to make room for present desperations. I greeted it uncomfortably, a new friend in an old friend's sweatshirt. It was all I could do.

Two months in, and I was back in the swing of the retail game. I compared coffee to clothes like apples and other apples. The long hours and the light pay, the ridiculous uppity attitudes some people had, the funny light conversations with customers, being told to smile—those parts were the same in both realms. However, working retail this time took a different mental commitment—a gnawing voice in the back of my brain kept telling me, *This is not forever, this is only temporary, but, hooker, listen—you need this NOW. You cannot survive without this.*

Hello. I am Alida. I work for the man for money. And now I get why those hippie beards call these kinds of places "the Man," because nothing defines my idea of the man more: I was doing something I wouldn't be doing otherwise *just to make money.* The man could give you sweet kisses on the neck in the form of required raises every six months and vacation time and some holidays off. Then the man could abuse you a bit because they knew you needed the cash.

So I rebelled in the only way I knew how. I embraced it. Twenty-year-old me griped and frowned her way through shifts, went to the back room and made fun of specific customers, slacked off on the occasions I knew I could. Now, I would smile so the job wouldn't know how much I needed it. I pretended to enjoy it. I chatted with customers, got told my service was stellar. I came in early and left late. I tried to be quick, started tasks on my own, mopped enthusiastically, expressed my desire for learning more. I pretended that this was what I wanted more than anything else in the world.

If there's something that retail teaches you, it's to push through the bullshit. You have bad hours? So does everybody else. People treat you badly? Yeah, that happens. You have cramps and you have to put away heavy things and it hurts your back? I'm sorry, but that's what you're paid to do. It's also a job where the *bulk of the people you talk to don't care about you.* I've gone to work the day after a big breakup, and if you screw up, you have to make up for it. You don't get a free pass for your own stuff. When it boils down to it, it teaches you who you are, and either that person scares you or it doesn't.

After six years, I was okay with being the kind of person who did something she didn't want to do, to be the type of person who did whatever it took to get to the end of something greater. This was the transition time that built character. I wasn't working a dead-end job, I was learning to be more resilient, how to stay on my own two feet. To be something like an adult.

★   ★   ★

As the train pulled into the station, I felt that familiar sense of relief. *The workday is over.* I meet a friend at a neighborhood whiskey joint, ordering my drink in the typical "I *realllly* need this" fashion.

"How's work?" my friend asks, because she assumes I want to talk about it.

"Not permanent," I say. "That's what." I change the subject, tell her about something I'm trying to write. I tell her how I haven't missed a loan payment in a while as the bartender comes back with the drink. I take out my wallet, not feeing a pang as I hand over my cash.

This time, I tip her extra, just for the relief of the beverage and the little luxury of feeling generous. I give her a smile that she doesn't return as she goes off to make a Manhattan for an impatient man in a tie, who is thrusting a sweaty ten-dollar bill in her general direction.

I feel you, girl, I think, as I take another gulp, stretch my legs, and watch a barful of people making ends meet.

On Panic, or Conquering Fear Like a Child

When I was a kid, I was very afraid of sharks.

Correction: When I was a kid, I was afraid of *everything* because I didn't have cable. My mother thought that any show that wasn't on syndicated television would rot my mind and make me slothful and ungrateful and bratty. As a result, I watched two television shows on Friday nights—Christian game shows on PAX network, followed by *20/20*. Only one of those put the fear of god in me.

You've all seen *20/20*, right? Various professional mustaches and shoulder pads spend Friday evenings explaining how everything in your fridge causes cancer and how everybody wants to kill your sweet grandkids. That was my mother's idea of great-quality television time. Every summer, without fail, *20/20* would have a "very special episode" about shark attacks. "Little Girl lost half her body BECAUSE SHE SWAM." The next year it was "Do sharks follow little girls around?" and then probably "Will the government start feeding little girls to sharks if they don't obey?" Understandably, I became terrified of these godless killing machines, thinking they would eat me, or at least maim my arms, which was just as alarming, because even from childhood, it was clear that I didn't have the vigor or the spunk to overcome disabilities. Deep down in my heart, though, I knew a day would come when I would have to meet a shark. Why would I be so scared of them if I would never have to confront said fear? Hasn't anybody seen Ralph Macchio in *The Karate Kid*?

Because my parents were nice people who wanted me to grow up to be the kind of girl who wasn't deprived of jovial family bonding, they planned a trip to Universal Studios when I was eight years old. I know some of you are squirming in your seats because you know where this story is going, and this story is going straight to the ride "Jaws." The Goliath to my David, if David wore Daisy Duck T-shirts and wasn't quite sure how to tie her shoes.

At the front entrance of the ride, a huge shark was hanging upside down. I nodded to my mother, the same way an action hero does when they are about to blow up a warehouse. I stuck my head straight inside the shark's gaping mouth, which was my version of "Fuck you," or intentionally dropping the microphone at the end of a rap battle verse. I was ready to face the black-eyed sea witch. I climbed into the tiny motorboat and sat at the best spot, closest to the water's edge, right with the selfish parents and the twelve-year-old boys.

If I were to tell you that I spent the entire ride crying, it wouldn't be entirely accurate. My sobs and wails probably sounded closer to the bloodcurdling wails of a thousand Civil War ghost soldiers. I looked into the eyes of the mechanical beast and tried to control my bladder, shoving myself so hard into my mom's arms that there is probably still bruising there to this day. But as quick as it started, it was over. I stepped off the ride and told my brother to *Shut uuuuup!* when he made fun of me for being such a baby.

"You don't GET IT," I told my parents. "I'm not scared anymore!"

I had seen one. I had looked my fear in the eye and now it was over.

I wasn't afraid of sharks anymore, I told everyone as I sipped an orange soda and watched the ominous rain clouds gather above my head. I had survived, I told everyone.

A lightning bolt flashed in the sky.

"Tornado!" I screamed as I buried myself in my mother's chest.

My parents shook their heads and silently watched their brave little daughter cry her way through another battle.

I have been fighting fears like these for much of my life. As I got older, I became intensely scared of killer bees, plane rides, and the ever-popular and absolutely warranted: clowns. I had never experienced fear of the unknown. That is because I can always pinpoint what I am scared of. Always.

Which is why, one unseasonably warm night in January, at twenty-three years old, I was shocked to find myself awakened by my own screaming. It confused me. There was no blood visible, no dream of being buried alive, just me, soaked in sweat. I felt like my chest was closing in on me, or the room was getting smaller, and my eyes could not adjust to the darkness. Something was very wrong.

It was the first time I ever felt like I was dying. Not the harsh, panicky nighttime realization that you eventually would die, but the very present, very likely possibility that any moment I would be "touched by an angel" and taken to the pearly gates of heaven or the pearly gates of sorry, nothing happens when you die.

I lay and waited. I kept living. It took ten minutes of pacing and drinking water to convince me that I wasn't going to die at the moment, but I still couldn't comprehend why my body was revolting against me this way.

Of course, the Internet would help me figure this out. The Internet solved all of my problems, except the one about how to leave the house. I typed "What if you feel like you're dying?" which was an odd way of putting it, but screw it, I'm not Doogie Howser or even Neil Patrick Harris, who I felt might have some insight because he seems smart.

According to WebMD, I was either already dead or having a panic attack. Great! Finally, I had leveled up in my never-ending game of "Who Wants to Move to New York and Embody His Neurotic Highness Woody Allen?!" My body had bowed down and succumbed to my socially anxious brain. Great job, body.

WebMD said you have panic attacks when you "displace

or are unable to handle [a lot of] stress." I call bullshit on this, WebMD. I was totally aware of my stress all the time. Things that made me nervous on a daily basis: that the deli will get my sandwich wrong and I will have to send it back, that somebody will get mad at me if I bump into them, if somebody will ring my doorbell when I'm home alone, if there will be mushrooms in my Mexican entrée, if my future husband will be someone who has posted mean comments on YouTube. . . .

I had always been perfectly capable of handling stress or nerves or panic. It had been my cross to bear for years, a cross that gave people like Jesse Eisenberg incredible careers and people like me a lot more sweat. When I thought about my life as a whole, though, I realized that that was the problem. *My life* was the issue.

Sometimes, when I looked at who I am and where I was going, I think of Tom Hanks in *Sleepless in Seattle* when he finds his kid standing alone at the top of the Empire State Building. Frantic and upset, Hanks looks the little shit in the eye and says, "We're doing okay, right?" The kid sniffles and nods and the audience is supposed to think two things: (1) yeah, you kind of are okay, and (2) good thing Meg Ryan is probably going to appear in the next shot to save them, because you guys are *so fucked right now.*

This is how I constantly felt about myself. Most of the time, the day went by smoothly. I didn't die. Sometimes I'd step on a piece of glass and bleed, or somebody is rude to me, but nothing too bad. However, when I think about five years down the road, even two years . . . I get tired. It seemed too much, like a climb up a very long staircase. How could I possibly reach any destination? How could I possibly make enough money for two more years of living in the city, or two more years of buying pants, or two more years, period? How would I be able to keep up with a job and not get fired, or start a career and advance in it? How could I possibly be able to progress? Where is my metaphorical Meg Ryan?

The most frustrating thing was that there was nothing I could do about it. I couldn't just "stop being scared of my future," so instead I had to deal with the frequent panic attacks I had—almost every night for the next couple of weeks. It made me feel like I was being dramatic. I wasn't starving. I wasn't sick. And here I was, pacing back and forth at night so I didn't have to wake up in desperate, clawing fear. My room-mates joked that I looked like a raccoon. I stopped going out as much. I started to dread sleep. I found myself very, very unhappy.

My unhappiness has different levels, depending on who I am talking to about it. If it's my parents or direct members of my bloodline, I must be *very* happy because I was not doing needle drugs or becoming a stripper. According to my friends in California, I seemed reasonably happy. To them, I lived in an area where the weather sometimes sucked, but how could I not be happy when I ate bagels and drank tasty tap water and rarely sat in traffic? According to my circle in New York, I seemed totally okay with being the creative single gal, always cracking a joke or making topical references and halfheartedly doing wellness juice fasts and whatnot. My best friends know my brain was a minefield of terrible guys I shouldn't be thinking about, existential moments where I questioned the universe, and slight insecurities about my love handles. But by all means, I seemed generally okay to them.

Usually, they were right. I've always been—despite my deep desire to become one of those writers who actually felt the immense weight of suffering—a fairly optimistic person. Even when I was kicked to the ground by some bad week, I'd try my hardest to wallow and found that I wasn't very good at it. I kept pickin' myself up. Now, I wasn't sure. I didn't trust myself. I didn't like that although I felt okay, there were parts of myself, parts I couldn't see, that feared some unknown thing I could not get rid of, could not run from, could not seem to stop.

The moment I started telling people about my panic attacks, they got really excited. Their eyes lit up. They dropped some fuckin' *knowledge* on me.

"Oh, hell yeah! I have panic attacks *all the time*. You've got to stop overloading on caffeine, and you probably need more than ten hours of sleep *a week*. Come on, Alida. Get off the Internet, take care of yourself."

"Jesus, Alida. Everybody gets panic attacks. Have you seen this economy? And come on, you live in New York City. You're not a New Yorker until you kick a cab, get mugged, or have an existential breakdown in a crosswalk."

Alida Nugent

"Panic attacks? My life is just one *loooong* anxious wait for death. Seriously, get used to it."

There was no pity—only camaraderie, an acknowledgment that most of us twentysomethings are pretty anxious about our lives. Come join the club, they all begged! The water is clammy and harsh and unforgiving! We'll all die in here!

My friends, well versed in the kind of screaming panic I was just getting used to, had some remedies. Because nothing I was doing was working, I decided to try them out, to varying results.

Things That People Suggested I Do to Ward Off Panic Attacks, and Results of These Experiments

1. Drinking

The first panic attack advice I followed was from a self-proclaimed expert in them. "The secret? Never go to bed sober," he told me. He was the kind of guy who drank a glass of whiskey every night before bed, something I both admired and feared, like people who still use AOL.

"And . . . drinking helps the panic attacks go away?" This seemed like a great way to jump-start that drinking problem I'd been meaning to get.

"Trust me. Alcohol will cure this. You just have to drink alone. Don't go out to those FUCKING BARS, Alida. That'll just make it worse. It's depressing watching all those idiots try to drink away their goddamn problems. Just do it all by yourself, with nothing but you and your irrational fears and your demons. Just come home and pour yourself a drink at the end of the day."

"My demons love the taste of gin, I think."

He rolled his eyes. "You don't drink gin, what are you, a divorced mother who is abandoning her children? Jesus. Pour yourself a glass of wine, or whiskey. So do that, feel yourself getting a little drunk, let your head hit the pillow, and I promise you'll get a full night's sleep."

He was adamant. I was getting debriefed like I was Jason Statham's tiny half-Latina sidekick who was just "along for the ride." I would follow his instructions to a T, lest I would DIE by some Russian sniper.

The Result

The day after our conversation, I went to Trader Joe's and purchased three bottles of Two-Buck Chuck, a loaf of French bread, and a block of three-dollar brie. I plopped my purchase on the counter and looked at the attractive-but-also-a-white-guy with dreadlocks, begging him to comment on either how very French or very sad I was.

That night, I opened up my Charles Shaw shiraz in my ratty T-shirt and Old Navy pajama pants. The sipping eventually eased into chugging from the bottle as I sat cross-legged on my bed, reading an Anthony Bourdain book. After a while, I started getting restless and began to do a very stupid thing: watch various YouTube videos of Adele covers. Obviously, I started crying a little bit because the combination of wine and

Adele is pretty much the biological go sign for releasing tears. Then, I began to smoke cigarettes out my window and look up a bunch of my exes on Facebook. Eventually, I looked up the ending to *Toy Story 3*, Skyped my best friend while crying, and couldn't get the wine stains off my teeth despite vigorous brushing. This experiment was not going well.

My roommates were waking up to the constant sounds of my padded feet going back and forth to the bathroom or to the kitchen to eat huge bites out of a small block of cheese. I drunkenly imagined what they would say during my *Intervention* episode. "Your addiction has affected me in the following way: You're being weird."

That night, I fell asleep with purple lips and dreamed about burning planes.

2. Yoga

Obviously, drinking before bed was not the way for me to solve my never-ending panic. Going to sleep to the images of planes going down was so *Garden State* of me, and thus exactly what I needed to stay away from.

A lot of people recommended yoga, which wasn't something I ever wanted to do because I hate to clear my mind, and also, I don't like anything Julia Roberts tries to do in *Eat Pray Love*. But my "rich friend who pretends like her dad doesn't pay for all her credit card bills" told me that she relieves her tension by masturbating or yoga. I have done one of these enough to know that sometimes solutions are fleeting and maybe you should get off your back and try yoga every once in a while.

The Result

It was 4 P.M. on a Saturday when I'm trying my damnedest to learn a pose called "Happy Baby." It was not. Going. Well. I rolled around and tried to come up with a soothing chant to get me through the class. *Guy who looks nice in suit, guy who looks nice in suit, beard, beard, two more seasons of* Community, *two more seasons of* Community. While this rolling around made me giggle, it also made me twist my hamstrings in a way that I do not approve of. I'm not a fan of physical exertion when I could be sitting silently like a slug, doing absolutely nothing.

The classroom was cheery and brightly lit and filled with mirrors, which are three things that do absolutely nothing for my concentration or peace of mind. All the women in my class were wearing Lululemon and smelled like tea tree oil or Burberry Brit—I had on a Beatles T-shirt and smelled like the bottom of my closet. They all raised their hands up to the sky, wearing silver jewelry they didn't lose at bars, looking calm, like they worked hospitality at hotels or retail at an expensive bag store. People who do yoga never look like they *need* to do yoga, or be calm, or learn any of that.

I tried to focus at the task at hand: clearing my mind. This was a hard thing to do for someone whose problem was thinking of a lot of things at once. I breathed and tried to remember yoga wasn't about Phish and granola anymore, but urban ladies who knew all their chakras and had clean bedsheets. I can be this lady, I think! It's not my fault *Namaste* is such a funny word!

After the class ended, one thing was clear: Improving the body and dulling the mind officially did nothing for me. On to the next one.

3. "Ignore the panic attacks and go shopping and continue to dwindle your savings because eventually, it will all work out."

The Result

HAHAHHA. This worked well.

4. Drugs

Finally, there was Xanax. Everybody knows somebody who has prescription medication available. Pills are often passed around like candy, but the kind of candy you hopefully don't want too much of, like Good & Plenty. I briefly ran over the idea in my head to go to the doctor to get a prescription, but that seemed annoying and like something I wouldn't want to do—find a doctor, go to the doctor, tell the doctor something, go to the pharmacy. Too many steps. Too little health insurance.

When my friend offered me a couple of her little white pills, I accepted immediately and with great excitement. (Note: Yes, I know this is a crime. Yes, you should go to the doctor, pay a co-pay, try to slip in that you have panic attacks or get nervous on airplanes or whatever it is you need to do. Get a prescription and fill it at the CVS. Buy some toilet paper, maybe a magazine, meet a guy there, date him, get married, live a pure life of legality.)

I should say, I'm by no means a "drug person." To me, marijuana seems like something you do in college if you have so much time on your hands, you want to fill those hands with Xbox controllers and Doritos because nobody thinks you're going to contribute to society while wearing that hemp necklace. Cocaine seems like an expensive way to act like a douche bag. Ecstasy is for people who enjoy having sex to laser lights. However, pills were appealing to me because of its simple promise: You take one and you function normally for a little while.

The Result

When I took my first pill, I felt the unfamiliar waves of nothing. I felt nothing but in the moment, the reading of the book, the gentle music playing in the background, the decision to put my hair in a ponytail. The world was no longer crashing down at my feet. It felt like . . . being normal. The Xanax had worked. Of *course* they worked, they're drugs designed to stop panic attacks.

Even though I had a solution, I wasn't really happy, because it wasn't really solving the problem at hand, the problem being that I was scared of my life. And to that, there's no solution. Death, maybe. But that's a little much.

When I was eight, looking a shark in the eye was the worst part of the whole thing. The climax. The part in *Gladiator* where Russell Crowe finally fights Joaquin Phoenix. The rest was just falling action. What happened to that kid? That kid who bravely stepped up to fear and said "Fuck it," right in its face?

Now, there is just the panic. The idea there might be something in the water, the idea that you might never find land, the idea that you'll never paddle anywhere. That's what was keeping me up at night—not the shark, but the swim. An ocean of bills and trying to be happy and the idea that you had no lifeboat, and that this stuff wasn't just in an amusement park in Florida, but a real thing one had to deal with in order to move forward. I could get through today, I think. And then when I get through today, I'll get through tomorrow. And eventually, it will be five years from now, or, as I see it, "a fuckload of tomorrows."

A shark never sinks if it doesn't stop moving.

I put the second pill down. I get ready for bed.

Lots of people are scared of the water. It was about time I got in, anyway.

Liam Neeson Is Probably the Reason Why I'm Still Single

For as long as I remember, to all of my friends and my enemies, I have been known as "the single one." It's a role that I have proudly owned for several years, ever since I broke up with a boyfriend who spent all of his time playing Xbox and asking for me to go pick up his Chinese food. Being in that relationship left a bad taste in my mouth (literally and figuratively), so I gave up on dating and put my energy into becoming a single-person expert, like Carrie Bradshaw minus a million *so this got me thinking*. I was the four-eyed spokesmodel for leading a satisfying and sassy life while waiting for somebody special; because, ladies, you don't need satisfaction from just *any* man. Even friends in relationships found me inspiring and talked to me about their love issues. Why people listened or took instruction from somebody who had not dated anybody worth mentioning in years, I'll never know. Oh. Yes I do. Because *people love talking about their relationships*, even to their very single, very alone friends.

And alone I was. Alone and available, the single friend you could rely on. Need a friend to be your wing woman? Call on me to be the wise-cracking, slightly rude Louise to your much more datable-in-comparison Thelma. Want to vent about the shitty thing your boyfriend did and don't want other in-happy-relationship friends to judge? I'll offer you the best advice, and by best I mean drunkest, and by drunkest I mean something heartfelt where I offer to punch him in the kidneys until he remembers to text you more often. If I were on a reality television show, I would wear a flowy chiffon top and say lines like, "I may be single, but don't count me out just yet!" or something else tragic and alcoholic and mildly hopeful.

Now just because I was never in a relationship didn't mean I was Julie Andrews pre–von Trapp family. I didn't date seriously, but like a lot of young women of this generation, I "hung out." I made out with people at house parties. I had month-long, uninvested flings with the kinds of men who looked like they went home and wrote things on their walls with Sharpies. Traditional dating, as a practice, was nonexistent to me. No Thursday-night rituals of meeting another investment banker who describes, in detail, the first Negroni he had in Italy. No Wednesday-night napkins on lap, hand-holding through cobblestoned streets, and a rotation of kisses by the subway. And you know what? For a while, this was pretty awesome. I spent all my time going to happy hours with my friends and licking my fingers in public and telling them about how I sat awkwardly on the couch to watch a slasher film with another tattooed stick who had mismatching furniture.

Over time, there were certain disadvantages to my lifestyle, like, I don't know, forgetting what it was like to have nice feelings about somebody. My heart was becoming as hard as a game of drunken Jenga: in other words, really fucking hard. On the exterior, I was totally cool with my single status, but deep down, I was beginning to think I would never love again and that my sexy underwear collection would start to disintegrate into a pile of crushed dreams in my top drawer. And, of course, my social interactions were suffering because of this. I was losing the ability to *relate to my peers* because I began to associate romantic relationships with drilling out the part of your brain that craves independence. Whenever people started talking about their dating lives, I would shake around like I was a forty-year-old dancing at a Florence and the Machine concert. The "Dog Days Are Over!" Get me out of here! A conversation might go like this:

Friend 1: Danny and I can never get TOO serious because he doesn't have an air conditioner in his house and I can't just have him at my apartment ALL THE TIME, you know?

Me: BLearrrppp bERRRPPP

Friend 2: I know what you mean. I just wish I would stop gaining weight from going out on an average of three dinner dates a week with very nice, responsible men.

Me: (Falls on the floor, pool of vomit around mouth, no-body finds her for days because nobody loves her.)

Dating, to me, was like the Billy Joel song "Scenes from an Italian Restaurant," specifically the long, beginning part that nobody wants to really listen to where he yammers on about various bottles of wine. It was for people who were willing to hang around guys who remembered things like when your birthday was or your last name. I was ignoring the part of me who desired that, replacing it with "What kind of amusing story can I get out of this guy I prefer to keep at arm's distance?" It was all about single-lady power! Feminism and freedom! Lackluster night leads to five-minute tale to keep friends on edges of barstools!

Which is why I was thoroughly offended when, over dinner, a friend of mine suggested, "Alida, maybe it's time you tried the whole online dating thing."

The whole online dating thing?! I couldn't tell if that meant that everybody was doing it or it was shameful and gross and therefore I deserved it in my cretinlike single state. Were people worried about how I was single even though I went out of my way to make self-deprecating jokes about it? I thought I was doing the best job I could of being the friend who didn't ever go out with anybody, so other friends could tell themselves "At least there's Alida," when they were particularly upset about being the only single girl in the world. I wasn't the sad type who pleaded for friends to find somebody for her! I was the one who handled being the third wheel like a pro, and that wasn't a badge I proudly wore so I could avoid vulnerability. Not at ALL.

I gruffly took a large bite of my hamburger, mouth full of gristle and medium-rare cow murder, and told her, "You can't SELL me!" Her suggestion was insinuating that I was willing to drop a piece of my pride on the floor and stomp on it by admitting I was in need of some lovers. Some company. Some hugging.

She chewed on a cucumber for what seemed like ten hours before finally saying, "Calm down, Alida. Online dating isn't a big deal. Don't get mad at me. It's not like I'm saying your life is some sort of modern twist on a *Cathy* comic. You're not pathetic, you just don't try."

Ouch. Now *that* was the way to go about it—using the most tragic heroine of singledom as a point of reference for my situation. If *Cathy* comics even still exist somewhere on the saddest of sad-lady refrigerators, there is most definitely one about her trying online dating. She would say, "Ack!" and get really emotional about chocolate and bathing suits and then try to meet guys online.

There were two major reasons why I didn't find online dating appealing: first, because their commercials were *terrible* and always featured Waspy New England-looking couples, and second, because I didn't want to deal with CRAZY AT-TACKERS, come on! Didn't the foundations of made-for-TV movies cross anyone's mind anymore? Sure, the specifics fade, but there are definitely at least twelve of them with these plots: Beautiful, innocent girl trying to be a nurse in a small town gets chopped up by attractive man she goes out with on an online date "just this once." Beautiful, innocent girl trying to be a dental hygienist in a slightly larger town gets buried underneath a construction site because she turned on her computer and just *looked* at a GeoCities Web site for singles. Those movies taught a valuable lesson that has stuck with me for years: The moment you seek solace in a stranger, a man wearing a boxy leather jacket will break into your house and chase you around before you have to kill him in a swelling conclusion of self-defense.

My friend was gently persistent. "Come on. *Everybody* does it. How do you think people meet these days? In the grocery store?"

Grocery stores. Bars. Dark street corners. Anywhere but the Internet, a place that primarily caters to lonely people biding their time.

She and I began debating the merits of it, a moment I had been unknowingly waiting for since I was voted Most Valuable Debater in my tenth-grade history class. "But I can find somebody on my own!" "But you haven't." "But I don't trust the Internet!" "Alida, you have a blog, and I've seen you post your home address on it, asking for people to bring you cheese sauce. That dam won't hold, sister." "You're right. If I meet my next boyfriend online, I will no longer have anything accomplished outside the virtual world. That would make me a weirdo!" "*Fine, Alida, I met my last boyfriend online. Can you shut up now?!*"

I almost choked on my own self-righteous spit. Whaaaaaaat? She didn't stop with her own relationship. There were more. My sneaky little friends who said they had dates that night with someone they "met at [insert a normal place to meet someone]" actually met their significant others through Internet algorithms that matched their mutual interest in lo-fi bands and a similar appreciation for visually pleasing book-shelves as a centerpiece for the home. Those bastards! Those happy, happy bastards. All this time, they were making me feel secretly bad about my inability to meet people, but as it turns out, they were just workin' the system that I had assumed was meant only for pedophiles and divorced women.

I left the dinner feeling insulted, but also a little intrigued. After a healthy dose of Facebook stalking, looking at these friends and their boyfriends and girlfriends who met through the Internet, I started to reconsider. Who was I to judge them? They all seemed to have normal, happy relationships. I should be judging myself, the cruel and loveless judger.

Maybe online dating wasn't all murders and Nantucket white folks. Everybody was online dating, and this appealed to me in the same way the whole "everybody was jumping off a bridge" thing appealed to me when I was a kid. WHY was everybody jumping off a bridge? Was the world ending? Was it a small bridge and would it just be fun? Do I want to live in a world where all my friends and family were dead? I had always secretly thought, *Yes, I would jump off a bridge if everybody I knew was doing it,* and this currently translated to dating trends on the Internet. Jump I would.

★　　★　　★

Like any worthy experiment, online dating appealed to me in that I could do it without ever getting off my couch. So a few days after the *confrontation*, I turned on the ole MacBook, ready to talk about myself enough to warrant a message from somebody else talking about himself. But what site to choose? Christian Mingle? Not with the dark forces on my side. JDate? Promising, but I didn't want to give any Jewish mothers a big April Fool's when they see how Jewish I look and how Jewish I am not. Match? You might get my dignity, but you're not getting my money, pal. So I went with the obvious, youthful cheap-person pick—OKCupid.

The creators of OKCupid must have sensed how anxious their users are, because their home page is reminiscent of a pediatrician's office. It's all warm colors and cartoons and soothing jokes to try to make the whole process more comfortable. It might as well have had a poster of a kitten that said "Hang in There." The information you had to fill out was asked in the kind of way a very nice madam might ask a john at his first cathouse. "You looking for a guy? A girl? Don't be afraid to tell me what you want, hon. Sure, it's legal."

I clicked "I am a woman who likes men," because even though they have been a source of headache for me, I do rather like the gents. This was easy! The cartoon lady then prompted me to choose a username. This proved to be harder to decide. I hadn't had to make such a life-altering decision on the Internet since my parents let me get AIM in eighth grade. Should I go with my old school handle, Chatterbox888? Should I go with the one my parents wouldn't let me get—ThisPrettyYouthIsAloneAtHome?

I settled on FritesandGeeks after twenty minutes, an insatiable hunger, and a little inspiration from the earlier work of Jason Segel.

Next up in the process were the all-important photos. How did I want my future soul mate to see me? A beautiful candid of me wearing the latest fashions, photo retouched by a guy with a very big task ahead of him? Dream on. I couldn't have a flattering picture of me taken by Annie Leibovitz even if I was in utero in Demi Moore's body. The dude of my dreams would have to put up with having Cheetos dust pawed all up and down his clothes, so I went with a picture of me shoving popcorn down my throat at a bar. Then another with me smiling widely next to a goat that seemed to be the same height as me. Let's not create any illusions right off the bat, here.

I was way more excited to fill out the profile portion where I could talk exclusively about myself, which is why people want to go on first dates, anyway—to talk about themselves in a very, very positive light. The person who you project on an online dating site is a carefully crafted version of you—it shows the person you'd really want to be and the person you think you *are*. I came into this knowing I would talk primarily about my love for action movies and graphic novels and horror movies, which is somewhat true. I *like* horror movies, but it's not like I'm a dripping blood Hot Topic model. I just want to be seen as the cool chick or the girl who all the guys are like, "Hey, she totally knows what a machine gun is." If I wrote something about how much I also liked makeup, I assumed I'd be judged as a girly girl who would want to cry into Ryan Gosling's mouth during *The Notebook*. I had to be both cool and datable. This was a problem, however, because to me, this is what datable is:

Girl: I'm wearing a pretty dress.
Boy: I love you.

I spent a lot of time creating what I felt to be the perfect image of myself: funny, cool girl who could take a joke and a drink. It didn't come across as well as I had hoped. In some sections, you really had to wonder if I should just marry a sandwich and call it a day. I closed my MacBook feeling okay about the whole thing. Now all I had to do was wait.

When I woke up the next morning, I had the same kind of dread that comes after a night of beer and dropping your phone in the toilet or eating six pounds of cheese fries. I felt vaguely embarrassed but also really curious to see how shitty and rock-bottom my life could get. I told my friends I had "worked really hard to seem charming," neglecting to mention the photos and overly aggressive use of Pitbull lyrics.

But lo and behold, I opened up my account to find eight messages from potential suitors. *All right,* I thought. *The underdog reigns.* But my excitement quickly turned into disappointment when I started to read these messages. It seemed all of their keyboards were *totes broken!!!!* because it was impossible for these guys to stop using emoticons and exclamation points. I wanted to send them all to a nice community college that could teach them grammar and words to call a woman other than "h0n." Granted, online dating makes you judge people on the dumbest, most petty things: syntax, why people think it's okay to take photos of themselves shirtless, love for movies with Ethan Hawke. Many of them are probably lovely people who go out and help old ladies and have great parents and are nice. But I had to judge these people hard because I was looking into the darkest part of their souls: the part that thinks that pictures of them wearing Crocs on a mountain or doing a keg stand on a boat were THE COOLEST PARTS OF THEMSELVES.

I realized if I were to have any success with my online dating profile, I would need to get really specific with it. A little weird, even. I needed to find the kinds of guys who wouldn't send me generic stock messages about how pretty my eyes are, because the guys who are interested in me wouldn't lead with a compliment about my face. They would quote *Arrested Development*.

So I made my profile a little less polished and a little more . . . *me*.

On a typical Friday night I am: Seeking revenge.

The most private thing I'm willing to admit: I talk about the movie *Pearl Harbor*, starring Ben Affleck, significantly more than other people do. I do not like this film.

First thing people notice about me: My four eyes, two of which are brown.

Six things I couldn't live without: I could just say "brunch" six times.

You should message me if: I don't know who you are. I don't know what you want. If you are looking for ransom, I can tell you I don't have money. But what I do have are a very particular set of skills—skills I have acquired over a very long career. Skills that make me a nightmare for people like you. If you let my daughter go now, that'll be the end of it. I will not look for you, I will not pursue you. But if you don't, I will look for you, I will find you, and I will kill you.

(That's Liam Neeson's monologue from the movie *Taken*, by the way, and something my soul mate would love as much as he does the speech from Bill Pullman in *Independence Day*. And if you don't think that is one of the most badass speeches in cinematic history, then you should close this book. You disgust me, but let's move on.) My profile was updated and fresh and much more me. Its purpose was simple—I didn't need to be bombarded by messages from a lot of people. I needed just one person who thought I was funny, who was also funny, and who might want to hang out and crack some jokes with me.

★   ★   ★

A season passed. I chatted with a couple of guys who weren't put off by my weirdness, but I never felt excited enough about our banter to go out on a date. To appease my friends who said, "You're not doing it right, *Alida*," I eventually decided to go out with the next guy who would meet me in a public place that all my friends would know the location of. This burden landed on Craig, a new transport to Brooklyn who had large-framed glasses, a nice face, and a respectable love for *Mystery Science Theater 3000*. We met for drinks, where I sat for a couple of hours, drinking gin and tonics, making small talk in a comfortable way that prompted me to sit cross-legged in a bar booth and tell him stories I knew I was good at telling. It was a very nice time. He was not a murderer.

Try as I might, though, I couldn't get it out of my head why he was there in the first place. For things I listed. For pictures. For five messages that barely skimmed the surface of the ocean of things to learn about a person. When we said good-bye, we hugged. When he texted me the next day, hoping to see me, I told him I would be busy for a while. He bowed out gracefully because there was no stock lost with the absence of me. I didn't tell anybody about my date other than "it was fine," and then disabled my account a couple of days later.

Dating online isn't for me, I concluded. I didn't want to spend countless hours trying to think of the right thing to say for a couple of hours with some guy who rated me on a Web site. For some people, better people who don't get so anxious in dim-lit bars and with new people, it is exciting and interesting. A hope perpetuated by lovely success stories. But not for this girl. I began to accept the truth about myself: bitter girl was a die-hard romantic at heart. Bitter girl was happy being single, sustained by a love of alone time and bad TV shows, but also secretly sustained by the invisible face of someone she believed she could fall for. The mere fact that I could allow myself to hope these mushy mashed potato feelings made my stint with online dating worthwhile, a reprieve from being blasé, the return of the girl who used to cry at YouTube wedding videos, even if she made fun of them afterward.

I think somebody is out there, sure, but I won't find him online. He and I will meet somewhere where I am already comfortable because I know everyone there; we'll talk for hours and drink till dawn and kiss under a streetlight even though that's a cliché. It could take months or years of waiting. But one day? One moment. One guy. One game changer. That's what I would gamble for, that's what I wanted, and admitting it to myself made the "single girl" not a guard, but an invitation. For some dude, some adorable goof who may or may not love Liam Neeson monologues as much as I do.

After all, the way I see it, it takes only one person to murder you. It also takes only one person to fill your heart with the kind of joy that slaps you straight off your high horse. For the first time in a long time, I found myself believing in the possibility of both.

It's Your Day, Now Let Me Talk

No matter how many times I listen to "The Sunscreen Song," nobody will ever call upon me to make a college graduation speech. For good reason, though. Twentysomethings aren't exactly known to be fountains of great advice. We haven't chewed all the stuff we're learning yet. We haven't paid back our alma maters in full. And some of us, ahem, haven't stopped wearing ripped fishnet tights on occasion.

However, this book is not a college graduation ceremony, and I feel like I have some worthy advice to give after a few years of being away from school. I have processed some things—things I would have preferred to have known about sooner. I would go as far to argue that most of this stuff is 100 percent right, which is the sort of overconfident statement that only a twentysomething would make. I'm not trying to say that this advice is totally unique or mind-blowing. Old people probably learned these lessons at one point, too, but now time has rotted their brains and made them obsessed with 401(k)s and mortgages and other things that make me wish I could put all elderly people in homes to keep them from discussing these topics with me. If it helps my credibility, though, you can read this in the voice of an inspirational geriatric. But read it, dammit, and pass it along to your woefully naïve friends. And hey, Emerson College, if you want, I can come back and rouse audiences with drinking stories and how I half-assed all of your papers during my spring semester of junior year. I promise I'll watch my language and won't make fun of your Quidditch team. Too much. Anyway, here goes:

Today begins "the rest of your life." The "real world." The realization of "Holy shit, my parents are going to stop paying my phone bill soon." It's supposed to be an exciting day, but I'm going to take a shot in the dark and assume that most of you are extremely bored and possibly hungover right now. If that's the case—congratulations. You will spend many mornings of the next few years in this very state, so why not get a jumpstart on it now? Sorry, parents.

However annoyed you graduates are to be sitting here—checking the pamphlets to see how many more speeches you have to listen to, wondering whether or not you should throw your hat up in the air, contemplating what hand to shake the dean of students with (it's the right—or am I fucking with you?)—there's another emotion brewing in you today that I'm going to ask you to hold on to desperately.

Hope.

I know, I know, you were expecting me to say "hope." Everybody here was waiting for me to say "hope," but, hey, all the crap television shows you love are chock-full of clichés, too, so I feel like you can stick with me on this one. By god, men, you are going to need HOPE, and a hell of a lot of it, to get through the next few years. Things are about to get a little weird.

A few years ago, I was sitting right where you are sitting. I had spent the night before commencement dancing to Vitamin C's graduation song in my underwear, drinking whiskey out of the bottle and celebrating the fact that I would never have to read SparkNotes, or sit next to the obnoxious classmate who would constantly ask the professor questions, or run into the guy I hooked up with at the only frat party I ever attended *ever again*. The next morning, I woke up too late to get a breakfast burrito, put some blush on so my grandmother wouldn't tell me how pale I looked, and headed to graduation, feeling excited and nervous.

When I got to the ceremony, though, I couldn't believe how bored I was. I thought graduation was supposed to feel big and important, and instead I was hot and cranky. This was a huge moment, I thought. Why does it feel like just another long line, waiting for something else to happen?

Then, they called my name. I heard cheers and knew my mother and father were grinning and taking pictures and my friends were whooping at me because *I did it*. At that moment, I felt a surge of something real, something exhilarating. A real rush of pleasure, like the way you might feel when you think about signing a new lease in a new city, or meeting the person you might fall in love with, or landing your dream job. And that feeling? That's the emotion I want you to hold on to—that surge of hope and promise and newness and excitement for everything the future holds for you.

That is because a couple of months from now, you will feel *frustrated*. You will receive your first loan check in the mail and wonder why you need to pay for something that you no longer receive. You will have trouble finding a job and will become jealous of others when they land one. You will not be able to afford the clothes you want or the amount of drinks you want or the vacation you think you are owed. Perhaps most depressingly, you will start eating more ramen noodles than you ever did in college.

And this is when you need hope for the future. This is when you will need to test your character much more than you did inside these four walls, when you need to buckle up and hold on to hope more than ever before. Your life will feel scary and gross and uncertain, like you will never have a safety net again.

Not so—you are your own safety net once you graduate. Embrace what makes you stronger, because while college made you wiser, real life makes you tougher. See what you can do with this. Never forget the high you got as you walked across the stage, not because you were graduating, but because you were excited for the things to come.

You are here because you want to do something important. You are here because you have a dream you want to achieve, and that is going to become increasingly easy to forget about when things get hard. *Do not forget why you came here four years ago and stayed till this afternoon.*

To practice not forgetting, I am going to give you a homework assignment. Obviously getting a homework assignment on the day you're officially free from academia is something you'll roll your eyes at, but I promise you, this homework will be way more important than any of the exams and final papers you did at this college: *Do better.*

That's it. Constantly try to do better. Push yourself to do better than you did the day before. I'm telling you this because there are certainly going to be times when you're not going to want to do better; you might not want to do anything but sulk. You think it was bad when you were pulling all-nighters in college? Don't worry, it gets worse.

Some of you will work retail after college. Some of you will get paid next to nothing to be somebody's assistant. Some of you will feel like your life is in the shitter, and you will wish to be back at this very college. Don't become stagnant—even if you're working at a fry station, the worst thing you can do with your life now is to become stagnant in it. Nobody is telling you what to do anymore—you are your own teacher, your own boss, your own captain. You have to constantly push yourself to get better, or else you will get stuck. You are too smart and too bright and spent *too much money* at this school to get stuck. Do *better*. Become a mental athlete. Push yourself so much it's sickening. Stagnant water is full of mosquitoes, remember that.

Now, here comes the point of the speech where I had googled "What kind of uplifting quote can I use so I don't sound so goddamn depressing." I know a lot of speeches have quotes in them, and I didn't want to disappoint you. However, the only quote I could think of was the one Christopher Walken gave in the movie *Catch Me if You Can*, about the mouse drowning in the cream until it churned into butter. That's a good one, but I'm not getting paid enough for this speech to grace you with my Walken impression.

I'll tell you why I don't want to give you a quote—quotes by famous people make you think that nothing inspirational will ever be said again. Quotes by famous people make you think that everything worth saying has already been said. That's not why we're here today. We're here today because you are the ones who are supposed to be saying those inspirational quotes—you are supposed to be creating and marking this world and changing this world you are about to enter.

Create your own shit. Be your own inspiration. Work your *ass* off.

You may have worked hard in college, but that's nothing compared to what's going to come. I am here to tell you that you will work harder now than ever before because you have to work with fear. You haven't been used to working with fear. You've been living in a little hut of comfort here at college. That hut is about to be eaten by Godzilla. Let me tell you something—staying up all night working on a paper about Malcolm X ain't got shit on staying up all night wondering if you will run out of money.

However, there's a good thing about the fear. The fear makes things more fun.

The next couple of years are going to be the best, most alive of your life. Now, I know they said this when you were graduating high school, and then they said it about the college years, but I think that is because life is always getting better. Really, the postcollege years will be some of the most fun you'll ever have.

You'll find people, friends, and family who you stick with not because you are in the same classes but because you want these people to be your buddies in combat. They will meet you for lunch when you are worried about having HPV or getting fired. They will be your lifeboat, your 2 A.M. phone call, your "I like you because you understand me and not because we are in Lit 101 together."

You will lose touch with people you thought you wouldn't, watch from a distance while these people get married, gain weight, lose weight, move across the country, and get new sets of friends you will never meet. But you will look at your pictures of them and remember the nights you drank too much rum with them and you will enjoy those moments immensely. You will know what it is like to experience true nostalgia—the feelings a Hot Pocket can elicit will be astounding. It will not be a bittersweet kind of thing, because you know that it's not as much growing apart as it is growing up.

There will be successes, and failures, and a lot of good and bad things. You will watch yourself and the people you choose to be with fall in love and get married, get jobs, get fired, get a terrible tattoo, have babies, get sick, get better, get worse, lose parents, grow older, grow smarter. Things will flash forward, pass before your eyes like the lights at a terrible nightclub.

You will feel more alive now than ever before, this I promise you. Grab this time before it goes away.

So when you are sitting here, in your last moments of being in college, do not savor them like your life is ending. Look forward to that next step because it's going to come anyway. When you walk across that stage, do it with your head held high.

Get ready to make a contribution. *Want* to make a contribution to this world, because I've already said enough depressing things and I don't need to tell you that you are going to die, but, hey, you are. So make your mark, dammit. Don't lie there on your couch and fester. Put on your shoes and step out in the world and make something happen. Take what you love, and try to mark your headstone with something like "I was here. I did SOMETHING."

So, guys, stop looking so bored today.

Wake up.

Welcome.

A Friend Sits on the Hitchin' Post

When I got my friend Karen's wedding invitation in the mail, I put it down on my coffee table and accidentally spilled nail polish on it. *Glitter* nail polish. Somewhere, I thought, Karen was out there choosing china patterns while her friend and peer was fumbling with the kind of cosmetic that children wear. I wiped the nail polish off and decided to stick to matte colors from now on. Hell, if my friends were taking leaps, I would at least take baby bounds.

The invitation stayed firmly in my hand for a lengthy amount of time as I noted the thickness of the paper, wondered how long it took her to choose its particular shade of green. Just moments later, though, I used it to write down my aunt's e-mail address, because, Alida, can you just e-mail her a nice little paragraph about your life? It only takes five minutes and I know that you are *always on the Internet and you are also a writer and this should not be that hard for you.* After an estimated eight minutes involving a quick summation of summer movies I thought my aunt should see, I examined the invite again and then lightly tossed it down on the table, telling myself I would respond tomorrow. (*Sure, Alida, that's realistic.*) It was visible for at least a day, but eventually fell underneath bills and the latest issue of a magazine we stole from our neighbors. Out of nowhere one afternoon, uncomfortably close to the RSVP date, I suddenly remembered its existence again. I waved the now slightly tattered, coffee-stained, glittery invitation at my roommates.

"Guys! Somebody we know—somebody our *age* is getting married!" We had never seen one of these before—a wedding invite mailed to us and not our parents, a noncousin affair we had to provide our own transportation to. I hoped they would shed some light on what we were all supposed to feel about it. Happy? Biological clock ticking? Filled with the prodding fear of dying alone? We weren't too old to be expecting them to come in the next few years, we concluded, but we felt too young to be receiving them now.

"Well, of *course* you have to go," my roommates said. "Do you think you'll have to buy her a TOASTER? Do you think one of our buds will get so drunk and make a speech? Do you think there will be *salmon canapés*?" My roommates had not been to a "friend wedding" yet, so I was the sacrificial pioneer. I promised to report back my findings, as long as my roommate Amanda came with me. I wasn't sure if I was ready to field this alone.

Karen was not the black sheep in the marriage race. She wasn't in the "total lack of surprise" category, as she wasn't super religious, or pregnant, or dying, or dating somebody who was dying. I rated her engagement at "small level of surprise" because she was very nice and very committed to Jack and also very committed to making baked goods. She was an acceptable, comfortable start to the inevitable domino effect of friends getting married, the first lilac bouquet in a series of lilac bouquets, the start of a storm of rice throws and tux rentals and Cancun honeymoons.

I have always pictured my own wedding. I realize that as a girl, the patriarchal society wants us to do this so we will focus more on the charming effect a bouquet of daisies can have and less about how much less money we make than men. However, we're all feminist enough here to understand that it is perfectly acceptable for a woman of my age to imagine a lovely field with food trucks and those lantern lights you buy at Crate and Barrel and bridesmaids in black polka-dot dresses. I can tell you how much I would like a first dance with one spin followed by a dance-off to Montell Jordan's "This Is How We Do It." I can tell you how I'm leaning toward red lipstick, as long as I find one that doesn't smudge. I would mention how I fully expect a bulldog in a top hat to be in attendance, but I don't want you stealing my idea.

I like thinking about the details, of the party itself—but as I grow older and I learn more and more about how marriage is a combination of assets and also I'm single, I find my own wedding fantasies waning. So in my daydreams, I'm more often than not thinking of someone else's wedding. I'd much rather envision the wedding of one of my good friends, because I very much anticipate attending a wedding of which I am an integral part. I like to imagine myself in an olive-green silk dress with a well-fitted bodice, showing support for a bride I had always known would marry this groom. I deliver a speech with my hair swept to the side, raising my glass of champagne to say: "When Amanda met her future husband, I couldn't help but worry if it would affect how often she would hang out with me. Luckily, she met a wonderful guy who would also, thank god, listen to my problems as much as she does. That's when I knew I could deal with this whole 'situation.'"

It always seemed like a good angle to make jokes at the beginning of a wedding speech and then ending with a teary-eyed exclamation of their eternal love. Not a dry eye in the house in my wedding fantasies.

Of course, I also happen to be thirty-two in these fantasies. Not in my twenties. That's because, in my head, you meet a guy after you've been through a bunch of other guys, when you are older and more responsible and able to consider adding another person to your taxes. Still, I could not stop the wedding-gown train of destiny, as there is no going back from the first marriage of a friend. You immediately become the type of person whose friends get married, and you have to start thinking about growing up and getting a pair of smart Nine West heels for occasions such as these. It made you seem *older*. I take that back: It MADE you older. And just like the thrown bouquet, it's gonna come at you whether you catch it or not.

I distinctly remember a trip to my friend Dave's house in western Massachusetts in the winter of 2008. Karen and I were on a train, sitting with our feet perched on the opposite seats, headed to the kind of parents' house where they didn't mind "if the kids drank, as long as they didn't drive afterward." She was sipping soda out of a comically large cup, picking at French fries because no college student can enter a train station without purchasing fast food. It is part of *l'expérience.* Her face was youthful and pretty without any makeup. Her midriff was showing and she pulled out a book.

"So this guy I'm kind of seeing. He gave me a book. *Extremely Loud and Incredibly Close.*"

"He gave you a book about September eleventh? Isn't that kind of morbid?"

"I don't know." She puts the book back, and I don't ask her to elaborate.

Then we proceeded to go to a house where we drank beer out of a large glass boot and I tried to drink out of a funnel and she put on a boy's fitted cap and we smoked a hookah out in the cold. She never mentioned him again, not once, all weekend.

Four years later, I got glitter all over the name of the boy who once gave a girl a book about America's greatest tragedy.

★ ★ ★

As the weeks go by and the wedding looms closer, I think about strange things. Like, for instance, if I married my college boyfriend, I wouldn't be able to remember the first time we kissed. I make bets on who will get married next. (My money is on a shotgun nuptial for one of my more careless Catholic friends.) And most of all, I wonder if people ever realized when a moment, a glance, a look, was the kind of thing that would jump-start the beginning of another chapter in their life. I was surveying everyone about this.

"You remember that night, right? The night at Dave's? She didn't . . . *know* then, right?"

Brittanie, my ride to the wedding and my friend for everything else, sighs, her voice crackling over the phone. "I don't know. Probably not. The only thing I remember is discussing the need for females to empower their sexual behaviors by getting tested. We were both very into the preservation of the female body at that time."

It is two days before I am supposed to leave in some sort of Honda death trap, driven by her, DJ'd by me. I have iced coffee in my hand and I am by the bodega, pacing.

"What are you getting them?" she asked.

"I'm just giving them a check. People our age don't need candles, they need money."

"Great, I don't have a checkbook. I'm just going to give them cash."

"Bee, we're not in the mob. Why don't we just give them a joint check or something?"

"Fine. I'll get the card. I *certainly* don't trust you with the card. What are you wearing?"

I tell her I don't know.

The next day, I spend approximately thirty minutes trying to find a dress that echoes the casual elegance of the invitation. I settle on a black floral number that, while sporting a terrific skirt, had slightly overboard cleavage. Wedding cleavage. I believe it gives me a youthful look, the kind of look that tells people *This is all happening to us very fast, I'm still twenty-three.*

I plan on leaving my hair down but doing my makeup with an extreme flourish. I put all my things in an old backpack and remember my underwear at the very last second. Heading all the way back to Westchester with Amanda to await the arrival of my ride to New Hampshire, I realize I have left my check at the bottom of my bag, where it will surely get wrinkled.

When I arrive at my parents' home for a quick stopover, our other road trip partners, Brittanie and our friend Shane have already arrived. We gather in the kitchen, chatting a mile a minute in between bites of spinach lasagna. Actually, we didn't really chat—we were shoveling bites of pasta and bread in our mouths like pigs in a trough or hosts of a Food Network show.

"Do you want seconds?" My mother is staring at us, and she can tell by the mouth shoveling that there is very little food in any of our apartments.

"Yes, please. I haven't had homemade food since last . . . uh, *week*, when I roasted a chicken for some of my foreign friends." My mother raises her eyebrows. I have thirds.

We spend three hours at home, and my mother tells me my hair has gotten longer and that my backpack smells like cigarettes. She tells everybody else they look great. I happen to agree that they do, although I also think all of their hair got longer, too.

My mother makes us take a picture all together, because she has one of all of us at graduation.

"It'd be so funny! You all look so mature now!" I knew that she would put this on the fridge. A fridge, I noted, that was a newer, nicer fridge than the one that the grad photo had lived on for a while.

In our graduation photo, we all smiled. In *this* one, we all made funny faces. The older we get, the less we care about looking good in pictures, which is something we only decide when we chose to look constipated in our pictures instead of smiling.

"I have to go upstairs," I announce. In my mother's bedroom, I take two bottles of hairspray and a tube of toothpaste, because I've obviously forgotten them. And then, to bed! I sprawl myself out on the covers, waving my legs and placing them on the bed frame. From far away, I look like a child. I roll around and bury my face in the pillow. For ten minutes, I fantasize, like I always do when I go home—what if I never had to leave and never had responsibilities and nobody my age ever did, either? The perfect age, I think, could be eleven. I eat my crust now, sure, but my legs are in a constant state of dangling.

I lie on my bed until my friends come up to find me, to tell me we have to go.

The moment we climb in the car, out of parental earshot, it has been concluded that we must buy whiskey. There was no question of anything else. Whiskey is the drink of choice because whiskey allows nostalgia while seeming refined and mature. You have to have a strong stomach for it. You have to take it slow. When one's very first friend is getting married, you drink whiskey. You talk about things like old loves, or things we have missed, or things we have lost.

We are adults who don't buy Old Grand-Dad, or anything in a plastic bottle. We are adults who go and buy Jameson for thirty dollars in a supermarket liquor store. We tell the lady at the counter she shouldn't sell the margarita-flavored gelatin shots. She tells us, yes, they are awful.

Then she ID's us.

For the car ride up, we put on *Space Jam* and sang it at the top of our lungs and put our hands out the window, and it was like middle school again.

We put on Alanis Morissette and sang it at the top of our lungs and talked about how we wanted to drink whiskey in the car but only because it would make the story better. But we didn't drink the whiskey, and it was like high school again.

For the car ride up, we put on Fleetwood Mac and sang it quietly to ourselves and all stared out the window and passed around a cigarette, and it was like college again.

We ate trail mix and split the gas bill, and it was like every car trip I've ever been on with friends.

★　　★　　★

I figured I was going to get murdered and tossed in the rather vast field that stretched far and endless by the Knights Inn near Easthampton, Massachusetts. In the true spirit of being an adult, the four of us had decided that we would not "crash" on somebody's mothball-infested couch, and we would rent a motel between the four of us like normal adults might do on the way to a wedding. This motel is like the set from every slasher film ever made. I think of a groundskeeper walking around with a shovel and waiting to bury us, people peeking through windows. I've seen horror movies before, and I know I am a Hispanic girl with two white girls and an attractive guy, so obviously I am going to die first. I scream when I enter the bedroom, because it's all retro carpeting and an old-timey radio and GHOSTS. Shane turns on the ancient television and pours whiskey for each of us in plastic cups.

"Here's to a crazy night," he jokes. We know the routine. In college, when the four of us had whiskey in our hands, we would stay up all night, listening to music, talking the old "What does it all mean" philosophical bullshit, and getting so drunk we'd eventually pass out with our clothes on, our teeth unbrushed.

All of us got into our pajamas, letting the ice in the whiskey melt. Somebody turned on *Saturday Night Live* and we watched it in silence. I noticed Bee and Amanda fell asleep.

"It's a big day tomorrow," I could imagine them saying.

I stayed up by myself watching a Seth Rogen movie on

television. I fell asleep with mascara on, making raccoon eyes out of me.

We wake up at 8:30 A.M. Shane makes us watery coffee, and though it tastes like the piss of a dead cat, I appreciate it. I do Amanda's makeup—gold shadow to bring out the green flecks in her eyes. Shane steams his button-down shirt. Brittanie tries to sew a tear in her dress. I model my heels. We all decide, while checking our motel room for almost-left-behind hairspray or bracelets or ties, that we look like presentable adults. Breakfast is a worthy reward.

After driving around, starving and anxious, we finally find a tiny diner that smells like we have physically jumped into the frying pan and rubbed grease and canola oil and lard all over our bodies. I stand in the gravel parking lot next to the guy on the motorcycle, putting on nude lipstick and tapping my heels. Brittanie sits in the front, wearing sunglasses and smoking a Camel Light.

The waitress literally asks us if "we're from around here."

"You going to a wedding?" she asks.

Then, she tells us about the wedding she just went to, a Harley Davidson–themed job where the groom got in trouble for refusing to put down his Twisted Tea in the wedding party photographs.

"I can see why that might . . . raise some eyebrows." I excuse myself to the bathroom and forget to watch my step.

I eat eggs sunny-side up on rye toast, splattering hot sauce everywhere, never feeling like such a New Yorker.

We sit in the diner talking—not about the past, not about

college, or George, who kind of got famous, or that time I hooked up with George BEFORE he got famous. We talk about our real current lives and our futures, in Philadelphia and Brooklyn and Los Angeles. We talk about how our jobs are hard and our dreams are even harder.

We tip well and we go to a wedding.

I am totally fine when I wave to the groomsmen, my friend Zac, a guy I constantly envelop in bear hugs.

I am totally fine when the music starts.

When Karen walks down the aisle, I'm not as fine.

I have a memory of me and Karen and Brittanie in the nook of our apartment in Davis Square. We lured her over with a large bottle of Yellow Tail wine. The three of us drank and talked and made fun of each other for hours. She was supposed to leave early and we ended up drinking the whole bottle. That seemed like such a long time ago.

Now, she was being walked down the aisle with her mom and dad. I looked at Brittanie, and we nodded at each other through tears, like, *Where does the time go?*

And then I laughed because I was still at that nook, drinking wine.

I had half a bottle left.

When the reception started, I found myself drunk off punch almost immediately. I stood by the bathroom line and chain-smoked with my buddies from college, even though none of us were smokers anymore. We stared at the night sky and asked ourselves how long we had been like this.

"Years, it's been. Years since we've done this."

We reminisced about the time we would sit outside the dorm room buildings and refuse to go to class and share sandwiches and wonder where we could get alcohol.

We talked about the time I fell in the garbage can, or when Greg lined up a bunch of cups of water in our friend's dorm room, and he tripped over them and it was mean and funny.

We talked about jobs briefly, about current lives in different cities, then got self-conscious.

Mostly, we talked about nothing. About the moon, about dancing to music, about the veggie burgers, about Karen, about dressing up and looking taller and facial hair and how late it felt.

Karen's best friend gave the speech I knew I'd give to someone one day. On some day, maybe not as far in the future as I had always envisioned.

Someday, the someday with no space, is what you say when you're eighteen and imagining your wedding, in all its aubergine tablecloths and fall décor. It's a faraway thing, with no need to wonder if moments will be the moments that will shift you. The someday that exists when you're twenty-three watching a girl you used to do shots with walk down the aisle to the man who would now become her partner for years? It becomes *some day*, two words, a kind of admission that almost everything is around the corner.

I'm not talking about weddings, really. I'm not even talking about love. I'm talking about change. I'm talking about change happening right now, no matter how much glitter nail polish or pencil marks you might rub all over the evidence. Two years ago, I used to sit with all these people and talk about how easy it was to use SparkNotes to get away with not reading a book assigned to you. Now, we wouldn't do that ever again. What the wedding did, simply, was point that out. It stopped time for a brief moment—put the same people who knew each other a while ago in a different place. Then you got to see how much you've all changed. How much time had passed.

But some day is still not here, and so I get up and drag Brittanie to the dance floor. It is, for six minutes of hopping and smiling, exactly as it had used to be.

On Finally Feeling Home
(or, a Love Song for New York)

When you move into a new city, the first sounds you notice on your first night are the police sirens. For me, they were a constant reminder of things my mother had told me—that I should be careful, vigilant, scared. My wired-to-be-paranoid brain eventually interpreted this as "everybody who lives here wants to take something from you," so I lay on my bed, frozen stiff like the corpse I would no doubt soon become. After a while, I stopped hearing them and heard other noises—the dog barking, the Spanish music that blasts every Sunday night, the drunk girl outside my window calling her ex-boyfriend. They stopped keeping me up and began lulling me to sleep. Now, I find the absence of noise unsettling, which for me, was as much of an "I belong in a city" badge as figuring out the subway lines. The first night, though, all I heard were the sirens.

When you move into a new city, you can't help but feel lost and unwanted. Most cities aren't very welcoming to begin with (urban development < cozy farmhouse) and you don't have to live in New York to know that New York is the stern patriarch of the lot of them. *Excuse me, I'm walking here!* It is a place where you plan on fighting both your goodwill and your personal demons, somewhere to succeed by scraping by for the chance of a bigger success.

It was hard to move to a place that I knew I would eventually feel very lost in, and I didn't do it because I am naturally thick-skinned. I did it because I am very thin-skinned and wanted not to be. I had visions of being a *real New Yorker*. I'd be the kind of girl who knew where every dumpling house in every neighborhood in Brooklyn was. I'd keep my coat on the chair so I could grab it quickly on the way out to meet friends for a slice of brick-oven pizza. I'd impatiently stomp my feet while waiting for the G train *because that shit never comes*. I'd put on my mascara when the train was making turns and keep my phone in my zipped pocket so nobody would swipe it. A poster girl for belonging.

As many beautiful things as New York has to offer, it is also a place where you go to feel smaller than you've ever felt in your entire life. This idea of the challenge is why I lugged my suitcases up three flights of stairs and said, "Well, this is the start of something very wonderful and very terrible." It is a place that allows the smallest accomplishments to become the biggest, for the biggest lows to swell into the highest of the highs. Making it is *making it*, and failing meant you might have to hang up your fighting gloves and move somewhere with cheaper rent. Correction—sometimes failing means

NOT moving somewhere else with cheaper rent, of letting the pride of simply being a New Yorker grip the better parts of your judgment.

There is no open-armness about city life, no kind voices to tell you not to take a certain route at night or where to get the best sandwich at 2 A.M. Instead, there is concrete. There are thick, crumbling slabs of it everywhere you walk, and maybe once or twice you will see a weed growing out of it and appreciate that it is there. The rest of the time you will just keep walking. Everything happens in flashes: There is the prominent smell of both fuel and garbage, which seems to have a miragelike presence in the summer, but the moment you walk by a bakery, you remember what it is like not to live in a place constantly surrounded by carcinogenic fumes. It's a brief reminder of old places you called home, of bread and toast and the people who served it to you. For me, New York is filled with fleeting thoughts you have for something you miss, followed by memory loss and the complete saturation of being a part of a thick, pulsing crowd that shifts toward no one common goal. You become part of a big, uniformed fish school with no one destination but an underlying thought: *Keep going.*

New York is motivated by not just moving toward something but also moving toward something in the fastest manner possible. Until you start to get your legs moving, you will always feel like you are lost. Every time I walked into Union Square or any other square, I would be shoved by old women with walkers and muumuus telling me to speed-the-fuck up.

Little children would knock into my knees, and I knew they were born here and I wasn't. The secret is to keep pushing, to keep looking like you are going to the most important destination of your life, even if that destination is just home on your couch to eat Fritos and watch television. *You* can know that, but they don't have to—you seem weak and disposable if you don't pretend like you're going somewhere interesting.

The first couple of times I looped around my new neighborhood to find the bodega with the cheapest soda and the best snacks and the fattest, most pettable cat, I felt like I wasn't supposed to be there, either. I had keys jammed into my pockets and I still felt alien. I got lost trying to find my way to the subway. I told my roommates that the two subway stops near my apartment were equidistant and it didn't matter which one I took. Wrong. You have to, of course, conquer a part of the city. For me, it started with the eight blocks between my apartment and the bagel store. After a month and a half, I knew the ATM to go to that had the lowest bank fees. I should probably have switched banks, but that seemed too permanent.

Brooklyn is the land of cash, of handing wads of crumpled bills to the extended arms of bartenders who shake their index fingers at plastic. "We don't take credit card here," they'll say, without even bothering to point out where one can find an ATM. Sometimes they will tell you this after they have slapped your drink down on the tiny cocktail napkin, and at least three times I had to ask my friend if I could borrow five bucks because I was fresh out. It's embarrassing in a way that I know it shouldn't be, but I dislike seeming like I don't know what I'm doing.

Living in a city eats your money in the most unique of ways. My phone breaks just when the gas bill gets more expensive. I suddenly decided I needed to "dress nicer," so I dropped fifty dollars on boots I didn't really need. I became more of a *spender* than I ever had before, because New York is a materialistic place to live, a prideful parade of possessions. You eventually get into a groove—the seasons change and you decide to rework the clothing that you already had to create "new looks" by wearing a jacket you bought four years ago and thought you'd always hate. You'll stop paying for cable or buying something like mayonnaise. You'll scrimp and hope nobody notices.

Here, people are more attractive than I ever thought people could be in person. If I get off the J train in some packed part of SoHo that only carries British and Japanese clothing lines I will never afford, I am surrounded with people who look like models. I'd never seen a *really beautiful person* until I moved into the city, the kind of photoshopped woman who can carry her three-thousand-dollar handbag on the crook of her arm. Like a praying mantis, they walk around the streets as if they were about to rip the heads off of their prey if you bumped into their ethereal, suit-wearing bodies. They aren't famous, but they *look* famous. You will feel plain at least twice a day, but every once in a while you will catch a glimpse of yourself in the window of a storefront. *Okay,* you'll say, *I look busy or important or like somebody thinks I am special.* This city is beautiful.

The subway is the most human contact you will have with

people. I have heard that there are lots of creeps on the subway, and every once in a while there will be some heavy-lipped drug addict, smelling like garbage and carrying bags and bags full of aluminum cans. I've never seen the guys who pee or the crazy grabbers, and for the most part, on the train that I frequent, it's just Latina mothers, Asian people sleeping, and toddlers crying about their juice. There is the subway preacher, yelling to the car that we should repent or *else*; there is the guitar player who ruins your iPod playlist and tips his hat to you, asking you for cash. Mostly, I just ride and blankly stare at the signs, or smile discreetly at whatever tattooed, plaid-wearing guy I fall in love with for three or four stops. There are always tattooed, plaid-wearing guys. I fall in love about ten times a day.

It's not just about having dreamy crushes on attractive strangers, either. There are so many people I come across every day that I always manage to feel something personal and real toward strangers. I do most of my living inside their heads, imagining things as they appear to them. The girl reading her book in the park, the little boy walking and eating a candy bar, the old man drinking a glass of wine at the sports bar, the couple having dinner. These are the people I form tiny connections with in my brain. *I like that guy. I hope that couple works out. I hope that man has somewhere to go home to*—it's a workbook exercise, a practice of human compassion I may forget when I am cursing out a particularly slow pedestrian. I'm also presented with real human suffering. People who don't have homes. Addicts. I don't always notice them, I don't always give them my quarters, but every once in a while, they will hit my

heart in a way I didn't expect. I don't want to lose that. It
makes me feel more a part of something, the kind of "Hey, I
guess we're all in this together."

There are places you'll call your own almost immediately,
a hangout joint that is just right, a store that you just know
you want to go inside. There is the small bar with the worst
lighting in the world by my house, the kind of light my
mother would yell at you for if you tried to read in there.
This is the place I go to for happy hour because they run a
two-for-one special and the bartenders know who you are.
There is the bar that is a six-minute walk from my house that
I go to only occasionally because it's thirteen dollars a cocktail
but they are really good cocktails. There is the place I go for
brunch because they put six olives in the Bloody Marys and
you can eat the same thing every Sunday and feel satisfied.
There is the place that I bring all of my friends because there
is the best fried chicken in the world, and there is the place I
go by myself to eat hummus sandwiches and be upset. Wher-
ever you are, it is your city, so set a flag down today, and try
somewhere new tomorrow.

I still wander the city and get lost, and I intend on doing
that for a really long time. I know that New York City is a
grid, and that Brooklyn goes from south-something street to
north-something street, but that doesn't mean I won't drink
and stumble somewhere I'm not supposed to be. I have no
idea how to find anything on Park Avenue, and I don't know
where to transfer on the F train to get to the L train, or whatever else you have to do once and never again. This keeps you

from getting a big head, and it keeps me from claiming this place as entirely my own yet, even though I still feel good when tourists ask me for directions. I always feign irritation at my own self when I can't help them. "Oh I *know* this," even if I have no clue. "Christ, I just feel so silly! Sorry!" I am always nice when giving directions, to prove New York's nasty reputation is unfounded.

There are places I can still walk around in and feel awe. When I stepped off into the South Street Seaport, taking in the slow waves of a place I never really travel to. Literal waves, there's water there. I hadn't heard the sound of salt water in *months*, I thought to myself. This is nice! Watching the Empire State Building light up in the colors of the rainbow the day gay marriage was passed in the city, the vastness of Times Square when you are up thirty floors, all of these moments are beautiful and surprising and wonderful. Later on, I might complain that I need to "get out of the city." You will, too, traveling with friends to some state close by to lie on the beach, to somebody's apartment in another city. You'll miss the city, you'll compare your city to other cities, and most often you never want to go back *just yet*.

I have met real friends here, friends I didn't know before I moved to the city who have no connection with any of the people I met before I moved here. These are the secret friends you cherish the most—oh yes, my Australian friend who I met at a bar, she's coming over for dinner tonight. Yes, that guy who lives right by Penn Station? I'm visiting him today. I am a capable person, capable of making connections with people not based on sex, who have lived in different worlds than me, and because of this I feel validated. You have never had to work hard to make friendships, and then you move somewhere new without the prospects of college classes or "friends of friends." Sometimes you'll meet somebody special to you, whether it is for ten minutes or ten years.

There are nights out that are uneventful, which start out disappointing and eventually become the relief of a still-packed wallet and a hangover-free morning. Not every single Saturday will be the Saturday that changed your life; not every weekend will mark some sort of wonderful, life-changing moment in the city that never stops drinking. Not the city that never sleeps, the city that is always down for another round in a place you promise will be good. I've taken the subway at four in the morning or six in the morning, sitting with my roommates, trying not to fall asleep. When you walk home in the light of day, you begin to question the little things about your life. I have done this on more than one occasion. (Although the general rule should always be: If it's past 2 A.M. and you are alone, please always take a cab.)

You will have moments that feel so incredibly CITY—the night I flashed drag queens who later fed me 4 A.M. truffle mac and cheese while complimenting my breasts comes to mind—and you will feel like you need to get more Jeffrey Campbell wedges and go full-on fashion-urban-glamour-puss. But some of your best nights might involve playing board games and ordering Thai food. Talking to your best friend on the phone. Going to a museum.

Not every night is a magical night in the city, and I'm still trying to find the balance. There have been nights where I have cried. There have been nights where I have laughed, have tripped on my heels and thought *I can't do this,* or gotten so overconfident in my place here I had to humble myself and take a breather. I have gone out drinking too many nights in a row, decided to stop drinking for a while and just sit on my couch with my roommate and watch *Mad Men* episodes, and times where I've taken a two-hour walk, only to be completely enraptured by the city I chose to live in. You get to know yourself in ways you didn't think possible when you move into a city. It's a beautiful experience.

You will accidentally make a blip: You will scribble something in Sharpie on a bathroom wall or lose your earring or give somebody wrong directions. You will have little victories—you will learn how to sew a button or get a dentist here you remember to go to or you will start getting haircuts on a regular basis. You will do something good for yourself.

I have become a presence in this place. A slight one, maybe, and one who will only grow as I learn to do New York things like wear a lot of black and check behind me when I am walking home late at night, but somebody who is somewhere in a big place that she has narrowed down enough to call her own.

Here I am, New York, I will stop saying. *I am here*, I will say instead.

I hope you find your "here," someday.

I hope you know you're already there.

Acknowledgments

Thanks to *Tumblr*, the blogging platform that gave me more love and attention than I deserve. I appreciate you all for following me, reading me, and letting me know that I am not alone in my odd endeavors to eat all the chips and drink all the whiskey. You have constantly made me strive to be better, which is something I'm not prone to do without incentive. For the ladies I have met via the Internet, giving me hope for the future—I think you are beautiful.

A special thanks go out to my friends: Grace, Natalie, Greg, Shane, Danielle, Sarah, Sandy, Lucy, Steve, Scott, Ian, Kelly, and Adam have listened all too much to my incessant whining about how much work it takes to write a book about how it's funny when I drink. To Amanda for giving me truffle salt and a good ear; to Brittanie because she gave me poetry and gave me teeth. To Grey Blake for making my Web site look nice; to Griff O'Brien for inspiring me, and to Evan for being my first follower on my stupid blog. Your support and drinks and love have not gone unnoticed. To the boy I suspect will still

acknowledgments

be around when this is published—thanks for letting me dance around in your basketball shorts to Rihanna. To three-dollar bottles of Charles Shaw. To cheese. To Emerson College and certain English teachers and Jimmy's Traveling All-Stars and yes, RAD!—without you I wouldn't have learned how much I loved to be funny, and without you nobody would have told me I should get better at it. To all of my buds for being there, here is the proof that I wrote a book entirely about myself. That's kind of weird, right?

To Kate Napolitano: your endless patience and occasional sandwiches have made you an angel to me. I couldn't have anticipated an editor I wanted to be my friend, and I can't thank you enough for fixing my grammar and my bad spelling and for still being encouraging even though I refused to meet deadlines. I hope we have many more books together.

To Andrew and Alyssa at Paradigm, and everybody at Penguin and Plume Books for thinking I deserve this book even though I'm a young shithead—what an appreciated gamble you took on a four-eyes like me.

To my family—Yaya for giving me her spunk, Nana for giving me her love of beer and her lack of height, Aunt Linda and Aunt Peggy and Fred and Titi Vicky for laughing at my jokes as I spill potatoes all over the floor on Thanksgiving. For my mother for a million reasons. For my genius father for letting me be a forever daddy's girl and trying to teach me algebra and also for letting me drink cold red wine while watching movies with you. For my brother for being my best pal and greatest protector and biggest role model. I am so lucky to have all of you.

And also for whoever is reading this—you're making my silly little dreams come true. Thank you, all, and I hope I haven't let you down. I'm glad you read.